This book is dedicated to
the people of the Chapel Hill Bible Church
who in receiving the Gospel of grace
have demonstrated and declared its peace
to their generation for the glory of Christ.

PEACE
SEEKERS

*Perfect Peace
for Imperfect People
in an Imperfect World*

A Forgotten Key
to Effective Christian
Leadership

JIM ABRAHAMSON

Torchflame Books

A note to the reader

Before starting the three sections of this book be sure to read the Preface and the Introduction, which provide a framework needed to fully appreciate the book.

Contents

Preface

Life is unfair and whining about it doesn't help.

Can a person find peace in this life without being perfect or living in a perfect world? The answer is YES, and in this book I intend to tell the story of how such peace is possible and accessible. But before we can experience peace, we must understand the profound way in which this is a spiritual issue more than a psychological or social issue.

Shalom

The Hebrew Bible (Old Testament) uses the word "shalom" (translated "peace") to capture the essence of the deepest desire of the human heart. In Hebrew, the root of the word can mean "whole" in the sense of "healthy", "prosperous", "complete", or "content". Related words in Hebrew are "Shulam" as "it was paid for" or "Meshulam" as in "paid in advance." Hence one can say that, "when it's paid for, then there is peace," or "peace has a price." This captures the Biblical teaching that stresses the legal transaction whereby reconciliation with God and others requires a just payment or peace offering. The promised New Covenant is a *"covenant of peace"* (Isa.54:10). The God of the Old Testament is "the Lord of Peace" (Judg. 6:24) and Messiah is "the Prince of Peace" (Isa. 9:6). Jesus is our peace (Eph.2:14) in that we have peace with God through him (Rom.5:1). But this idea makes an assumption—there is something in this world that is out of sink or fallen from grace and needs redemption before "shalom" can be experienced.

Shame and Blame

Even though past cultures may have been more in touch with personal shame and responsibility, both the past and the present are in agreement—there is injustice, anxiety, bitterness, and a general lack of peace. We just have different senses of where the problem originates and how it should be addressed. This book is for imperfect people seeking peace in an imperfect world. What I intend to argue in this book is that personal peace has more to do with how we see and respond to the cross of Christ than with the changing of our worldly circumstances (personal imperfections and the imperfections of our world). Christ IS our peace. He is not simply the one showing and enabling us to find peace through personal moral rehabilitation and social reform.

"Mistakes were made but not by me." These words capture a trend in modern Western culture. We are trying hard to convince ourselves that most if not all of our problems with inner anxiety and unrest come from the failure of our environment to cultivate and maintain adequate support for us. We have come to believe that the key to inner peace rests with the changing of our environment. We expect God to bring peace to our souls by changing the circumstances of life so as to bring about the "desires of our heart"—a great marriage, good health, prosperous and fulfilling career, the respect of others, etc. We have re-pressed our shame and tried to remove our pain by casting blame on something apart from our personal failures. It's not that we believe we are perfect but rather that we see our imperfection as not the problem. We see ourselves as victims in some sense. In many ways we have moved from a shame based culture to a blame based culture. We have lost hold of a deep sense of personal responsibility and the shame that goes with it, while adopting a culture of personal rights and entitlement. We have come to believe that our lack of peace is linked to someone else's lack of responsibility. Others did not do their part. They were not there for us to make things right. We believe that our problems rest with the delinquency of our mate, our parents, our kids, our boss, our government, our church, Satan, anyone but us. To make matters even worse, we expect God to bring us peace by changing our outer environment.

Ethics of the Soul

I want to look at the grace of God in Christ as it impacts our inner life and its responses to the outer world. I realize that we fail to live perfect lives, and we fail to find perfect environments. But I also realize it is not our performance or our circumstances that stress us. It is the inner processing of our broken lives and world that burdens us. We have a sense of "ought" that seems hardwired in our souls, leaving us with a sense of falling short of what we should and could be. It leaves us with a deep sense of shame and alienation from ourselves, others, and God. By the same token, we do not have an equally powerful sense of being able to rectify our condition. We may have the desire to change but not the power to do so. *Peace Seekers* is the first of two books, the second being *Peace Makers*. The first book is a vital foundation for the second. The second is a necessary completion of the first. I contend that peacemakers must first be successful peace seekers. Once we have found personal peace, we are then equipped to be makers of peace in relationships where we express what we have experienced.

Not Light Reading

This book is not light or easy reading. *Peace Seekers* is written to those who are comfortable thinking about ideas, reflecting on life, and engaging seriously with their faith. It will challenge you to think, reflect, and engage with ideas that may be new and deeper than your comfort level. This book is cognitively oriented but not scholarly or academic. There are no notes or references but many Biblical citations. *Peace Seekers* is intended to be personal but not sentimental, intellectually serious but not academic, deep and broad, but at the same time practical and specific. The book is best read with an open mind, an open Bible, and enough time to patiently reflect on its message.

Who Should Read this Book?

This book is written for Christians who live with a deep sense of duty that they have not, will not, and cannot satisfy. In desperate attempts to salvage self-respect they often deflect attention away from self and onto outward circumstances or causes. This is a book for moral convicts, not spiritual outlaws. This is a book for people who are in spiritual prison or fear that they are on probation before God. To borrow an image from Jesus' parable of the Prodigal Son (Lk.15) this book is written to the shameful prodigal not the self-righteous older brother.

Three groups of people will profit from reading this book. I am writing to help those who need guidance in experiencing and expressing the grace of God. I am also hoping to assist those who want to minister to them. These will be the primary audiences that I have targeted. But there is a third audience that can profit from these pages. It is those who want to understand the dynamics of effective Christian leadership. Leaders must be peace seekers.

Why is this book a Dangerous Book?

The book you are about to read may seem on the one hand idealistic and on the other hand dangerous—because its message can be misunderstood and abused. But the radical love and grace I will so often reference is Paul's message, which he identified and defended as the Gospel. Paul recognized that if his readers correctly understood his radical teaching on God's grace, they would logically ask the question, *"Should we sin that grace may abound?"* (Rom.6:1.) In response to this question Paul does not exhort his readers to recommit their lives to discipline under the moral laws of God; he rather exhorts them to live as those who have a wonderful new identity being fully justified children of God through faith expressed in their baptism. This suggests that what many of us may need is not a return to law but a better understanding of grace.

But isn't the modern church giving too much attention to grace? Don't we need a revival of law and order, fear of judgment, and moral discipline? In spite of all that has been said and penned on the Grace of God, it is still misunderstood, seldom experienced, and too rarely demonstrated. Because it

4

is often resisted, it must be a persistent point of emphasis in the Christian's life and message. But it must be framed and modeled in ways that permit its power to transform our lives and the lives of all who meet us.

Jesus' prayer for his followers in John 17:26 is that *"the love wherewith Thou didst love me may be in them."* It is the infusion of this love from God that motivates the changing of our lives and the writing of this book. When we know God loves us, when we know we are significant and secure as His children, and when we sense His love for those around us; we are transformed. That love is experienced as we grasp the story of God's grace in Christ.

How Is this Book Structured?

Three biblical stories that depict God's love and grace provide the structure of this book. Each story features a contrasting pair of individuals. First, we look at two builders—Foolish and Wise in Matthew 7. The Wise Builder puts himself under the Law of Moses and is broken by it. The Foolish Builder does not abide by the law but redefines the law in order to manage its demands and never comes to see his need for Christ. Second, we look at two mothers—Hagar and Sarah in Galatians 4. They represent two contrasting spiritual covenants that will help us understand our legal relationship with God. Those under the New Covenant are free from the condemnation of the law while those who live under the Old Covenant continue to be condemned by it. Third, we look at two fathers—Abraham and Satan in John 8. Their stories will teach us the relationship between faith and grace. The righteousness that satisfies the demands of a perfectly holy God is not the righteousness of ethnic heritage or moral discipline but of faith (Jn.1:12-13). Our hope is in God's work for us, not His work in or through us.

In a second book, *Peace Makers,* we will observe the story of two sisters—*Mary and Martha* in Luke 10. They will help us see the relationship between listening, worship (rest), and work in the context of grace. From there we will move to the story of two brothers—*the prodigal and his brother* in Luke 15, where we will examine the dynamics of repentance and grace. Finally we will look at Matthew 18 and see two lenders—*one gracious and the other unmerciful*. They will help us see the relationship between grace and graciousness.

We will begin each of the three sections in this book with an introduction and a self-test designed to prepare the reader to appreciate the chapters that follow. Each section will include a chapter(s) dealing with a step to experiencing and expressing grace and peace and also a chapter(s) addressing an obstacle to grace and peace. At the end of most chapters will appear a series of application responses and/or discussion questions. The section heads should be read before the chapters that follow in each section.

The Message of this Book in a Nutshell

The argument of this book can be summarized by drawing attention to three steps to strategic peace with God.

> *Step #1* The **Spirit of Holiness** - taking seriously Jesus' call to holiness and being broken by the law of God.

> *Step #2* The **Spirit of a New Covenant** - moving our eye away from our performance and onto what God has done for us in Christ so that we can see ourselves as justified before God apart from our imperfections.

> *Step #3* The **Spirit of Faith** - receiving the gift of Christ's righteousness by faith. It is a righteousness that is first *for* us and then is also *in* and *through* us.

There are also three obstacles to peace with God.

> *Obstacle #1* A **Lawless Spirit** - building a foundation of self-sufficiency that does not understand or willfully rejects the just demands of a holy God.

> *Obstacle #2* A **Legalistic Spirit** - inviting us to live under the law will keep us anxious, bitter, or proud.

> *Obstacle #3* An **Independent Spirit** - looking for hope in anything and everything but Christ.

Introduction

To sin is man's business.
To justify sin and sinning is the devil's business.
To justify sinners is God's business

In the late 1700s a British slave trader by the name of John Newton struggled with deep moral dissonance—torn between his profession as a slave trader and his conscience as a man born in the image of God. In his search for peace he became a Christian and not only found rest for his soul, but he also began a crusade to abolish the slave trade. He became a peacemaker. Newton's faith and freedom from inner turmoil inspired his penning perhaps the most famous hymn in history, *Amazing Grace.*

Amazing grace! How sweet the sound
that saved a wretch like me!
I once was lost, but now am found;
was blind, but now I see.

'Twas grace that taught my heart to fear,
and grace my fears relieved;
how precious did that grace appear
the hour I first believed.

Newton mentored a young Christian poet and hymn writer, William Cowper, who penned these lines,

There is a fountain filled with blood,
Drawn from Emmanuel's veins,
And sinners plunged beneath that flood
Lose all their guilty stains.

Unlike Newton Cowper spent most of his Christian life in deep depression going in and out of sanity, fearing he was damned to hell. To be sure Cowper's depression was a complex problem that involved both spiritual and physical factors, but the fact that both men were Christians did not assure both would experience the peace that was available to them in Christ. Not all Christians are successful peace seekers nor are they peacemakers. God's grace is the door to peace seeking and peacemaking, and to understand the relationship between the grace of God and the peace of God is our objective as we read this book. As we look at three New Testament stories, we will unlock "the sweet sound" of the grace that sets the soul free to know a peace the world cannot give or take away because it does not depend on our performance or our circumstances.

The Perfect Storm

Three powerful forces converge in the American experience—first, a performance based secular culture that penalizes and rewards people on the basis of their productivity; second, a religious sub-culture that is idealistic, perfectionist, and narcissistic; and third, sinners who are powerless to meet the demands of their conscience but obsessed with trying. The results can be devastating. The shipwreck is seen in a flood of personal psychological guilt, fear and anger expressed in toxic relationships, and social conflicts on personal, national, and international levels. The problem is not helped as people are exhorted to embrace false hopes for perfecting their environment or their performance in it. This book takes a different perspective and attempts to show how the good news of the Cross of Christ offers peace to imperfect people in an imperfect world.

> ### A point to ponder
> The Christian life is not about DO
> It is about DONE.

The Christian life is not about "do;" it's about "done." And it is not about "achieving" but about "being." The Good News of the Christian message does not center on an ethical challenge to *make* peace with God, our neighbor, and our own souls. Peace with God is won for us, offered to us, experienced by us, and ultimately expressed through us. Peace is the root of Christian living. Christian living is not the root of peace. We will not be peacemakers until we first are successful peace seekers. As peace seekers we will not find peace until we understand and receive the grace of God in Christ.

Distinguishing the Role of Christ from the Role of the Spirit

We must not confuse the ministry of Jesus and the ministry of the Holy Spirit. Jesus is a *Surrogate* (substitutionary sacrifice) while the Spirit is a *Paraclete* (helper / comforter). Reconciliation with God requires a purification of life that is only possible by what Christ has done FOR us and not by what the Spirit does IN and THROUGH us. The role of the Spirit is to first teach us the hope that is in Christ and to comfort us with that hope in this life.

Many Christians make one of two mistakes with respect to the role of the Spirit. First, they see the Spirit as instrumental to purifying them in this life so that they can be justified before a holy God. It is true that the Spirit empowers us to be Christ followers, but he does not produce the holiness needed for justification. Second, they fail to see the Spirit as a Helper in this life. They tend to overstate or understate the Spirit's role in living the Christian life. The Christian life is to be lived by us with the HELP of the Holy Spirit and not by the Holy Spirit apart from our human effort and involvement. We are not passive but active participants with the Spirit. On the other hand we are not reconciled with God by the way we live our lives in the flesh OR IN THE SPIRIT. We are reconciled with God by the work of Christ as our substitutionary sacrifice. The Spirit's primary work is to reveal and remind us of the finished work of Christ and to install his peace and power in us. As a helper the Spirit gives us power and guidance but even more so comfort and encouragement.

> ## *A point to ponder*
>
> Christ is a surrogate (substitute).
> The Holy Spirit is a paraclete (helper)
> not vice versa.

Confused, Cynical, and Cruel

In nearly 30 years of pastoral experience with one congregation and after working as a church consultant across several Christian traditions, I have made three observations concerning church-going people and their struggle with holiness, idealism, and shame.

First, people are confused. They are confused because of what they sense are conflicting messages from the Bible. They are asking, "Are we accepted by God or are we on probation with Him?" Second, they are troubled because of conflicted experiences and expectations in living the Christian life. "Why is there such a gap between what we expect and trust God for and what we experience and see in this life?" "Have we misunderstood the Bible?" "Why do we sometimes feel and act as though Christ's power is not working in us or in those around us?" "How can we keep from becoming cynical with life when God doesn't seem to follow His own rules or keep His promises?" For example, if God asks us to love our enemies unconditionally, why does He not accept His enemies unconditionally? Third, people are also confused because of mixed messages from the Christian community. They hear the message of grace, but they too often fail to see or experience it in their relationships within the church. "Why do we sometimes feel more acceptance and love from people outside the faith than from those inside the church?" This confusion is an intellectual or head problem.

Second, I observe that people are stuck and cynical. They want to change but feel powerless to do so. It's not that they don't have some idea of what God expects of them, but rather that they lack motivation or freedom to do it. They feel powerless to do and be what they should. This powerlessness can lead to cynicism, withdrawal, low self-image, and depression. They doubt God's love which they sense is the key to experiencing His power. Unlike the first problem, which is centered in the mind, this second problem seems to be a heart issue. People do not sense in their heart the love and power of God and thus feel stuck in the mire of cynicism, complacency, or rebellion.

Third, I observe that people don't act graciously. They may be able to explain the meaning and importance of grace, but their relationships are self-protective, self-destructive, punitive, and even cruel. They make God's grace hard to understand for others because they do not provide through their own lives a visual aid. They do the very kind of thing that they despise so vehemently in the lives of others. The person who hates to be misunderstood too easily impugns the motives of others. The person who was neglected and abused too often neglects and abuses. The person who hates to be manipulated too often withdraws, fails to communicate, or lies. The person who wants to hear more of God's grace feels no responsibility to sacrifice self-interest and be gracious to others. People who have been hurt tend to hurt other people. This is a hands (action) problem. We behave in ways we should not.

The Uniqueness of Christianity

How does Christianity address the human dilemma? Of the major world religions Christianity is unique in that it is rooted not in an ethical system, a philosophy of life, an emotional experience, or a social order but rather in the person and work of an individual in history—Jesus Christ. The writers of the New Testament Epistles are obsessed with Jesus—as they define the Christian Gospel and its implications for humanity. But we must note that it is not the high ethical teaching of Jesus that is the focus of their attention. Nor is it the political implications of his ministry that capture their hearts. Neither is it the many miraculous

11

signs and wonders that would become the basis of their message. The Epistles are virtually void of direct references to Jesus' teaching and wondrous works. He is seldom quoted in the Apostles' letters, and the many miracles he performed are not referenced in their writings. What then was the focus of their obsession with this man?

It is the crucifixion and resurrection of Christ that gets the attention. When Christians around the world worship, they do so not with a basin and towel commemorating humble service of others. They do not worship before a tablet of commandments guiding their ethical behavior. They worship at the foot of a cross and with bread and cup commemorating the sacrificial death and anticipated return of a resurrected Lord.

The late Roman Catholic archbishop, Fulton J. Sheen, in his excellent book, *Life of Christ,* notes that Jesus' claims to be the only begotten Son of God are not unique; for history has seen others make similar claims. Sheen argues in his first chapter that Jesus comes with four unique credentials. One, his coming was pre-announced. Even the Magi of the East knew of his coming (Matt.2). Plato and Socrates spoke of the *Logos* and the Universal Wise Man "yet to come." Two, his coming impacted history with such force that it split it into two (recognized around the world) periods—one before his coming (BC) and one after (AD). No other religious leader did this. Three, he was more than just a good man. It cannot be said that Jesus was just like other religious leaders, a great teacher or model of moral virtue. Good men do not lie, and Jesus claimed to be more than a man. He claimed to be "*the way the truth and the life.*" (Jn.14:6). He acted with the authority of God—forgiving sins (Mk.2:7). He made himself to be equal with God the Father (Jn.10:31-39) and accepted the worship of man (Matt.2:11, 14:33, 18:1, 28:9). No human Hebrew prophet would ever do such a thing.

But it is the following (fourth) reason that is of special attention for our consideration in writing this book.

Of all the religious leaders in history, Jesus is unique in that he alone came for the purpose of dying. His ethical teachings though great are not distinct in kind from the Jewish tradition of his upbringing. His miraculous deeds, though dramatic indications of his spiritual authority, are not the basis of the Christian gospel message. When John the Baptist announced the beginning of Jesus' earthly ministry, he did so with a view to its climactic end, *"Behold the Lamb of God that takes away the sin of the world."* (Jn.1:29). Throughout Jesus' earthly ministry he repeatedly spoke of "his hour that had not yet come"—a clear allusion to his crucifixion. It was as though the cross cast a shadow back over his entire life. The apostles in their writings were obsessed with Jesus, but it was not his life, teaching, or miracles that got their attention. It was his death and resurrection that became the foundation for their theology. Jesus' death and subsequent resurrection would define his place in history. It would be the essence of the unfolding gospel of the Christian faith. It would be the hope of all who by faith would receive and apply its gifts to their lives. It would be the key to peace on earth and goodwill toward man. And it is the foundation for the message of this book.

A point to ponder

Of all the world's religious leaders
Christ is unique in that he came
for the purpose of dying.

To appreciate the Christian story we must embrace three truths. First, we must embrace the full moral weight of God's holy law, which means that we must be broken before God and recognize the need for personal redemption. This truth leads us to the grace of God in Christ.

Second, we must embrace the freedom from condemnation that is embedded in the New Covenant of grace. This is something we must be taught. It is not something that we experience apart from hearing and believing the Gospel story. The "New Perspective on Paul" (NPP), which is popular in some evangelical circles, seems to miss this point. The NPP views the Lordship of Christ over all nations with the inclusion of Gentiles and Jews in one body as the central concern of Paul. While reconciliation between Jew and Gentile is important, it is not the heart of the Gospel, which is focused on the reconciliation of sinners who are alienated from a holy God by their sin. Theological "Justification" before God is best understood in the context of possessing the holiness needed for fellowship with a holy God who created us to bear His image. This leads us to the third and final point.

Third, we must embrace the grace of God by faith. Inheriting the blessings of the grace of God won for us in Christ takes place through faith. The Holy Spirit's role is to help or assist us in understanding the Gospel and living out the life of Christ. The three sections of this book will unpack each of these three truths as we look at the story of two builders, two mothers, and two fathers. We now turn to the story of two builders – the relationship of grace to holiness.

The Apostle Paul's letter to the Romans is his magnum opus, his foundational statement of the Gospel. He starts his letter with a stinging proclamation of the judgment of a holy God on all mankind—"*For the wrath of God is revealed from heaven against all ungodliness and unrighteousness of men who suppress the truth in unrighteousness.*" (1:18) But note how the letter ends— "*The grace of our Lord Jesus Christ be with you all Amen.*" (16:24). The path from God's holy wrath to the grace of Christ is the Gospel story. It is the path to peace.

Section I

Grace and Holiness

The Story of Two Builders:
Wise and Foolish

The Peace of God cannot be separated from
the Holiness of God

Is Christianity the only way to peace with God? The answer to that question depends on how you answer another question— What is wrong with this world and what is the nature of human brokenness? Put another way—Why do we seek and struggle to find peace? Why do we die? Answering these questions will enable us to appreciate the significance of Jesus and the unique claims of Christianity.

If there is one theme crying out from the pages of the Bible, it is this, *"Holy, holy, holy is the Lord God Almighty."* The Old Testament story is consumed with this holiness theme starting with the Creation narrative, which separates God from His creation (unique in ancient culture). Holiness is seen in the expulsion of Adam and Eve from the garden because of their sin. It is followed by the story of Noah and the judgment of human evil with a great flood. It extends to the exile of Israel to Assyria and then Babylon for the same reason. Holiness is the basis of the Law of Moses with its moral demands and atoning sacrifices. It is a major theme in the message proclaimed by the O.T. Prophets and Poets. Note these words from Psalm 15.

> *1 O LORD, who may abide in Your tent?*
> *Who may dwell on Your holy hill?*
> *2 He who walks with integrity, and works righteousness,*
> *And speaks truth in his heart.*
> *3 He does not slander with his tongue,*
> *Nor does evil to his neighbor,*
> *Nor takes up a reproach against his friend;*

15

If a person reads the New Testament in the light of the Old, which the early Christians certainly did, then the calling and purpose of the ministry of Jesus and his Apostles becomes unmistakably clear. It is the call to reconciliation with God through holiness. Peace with God is conditioned upon perfect holiness. Without separation from all sin (holiness), no one will see God. Jesus said that unless a person's holiness exceeds that of the Pharisees (Matt.5:20), there will be no peace with God. If we violate one part of the law, we are guilty of disobedience to all of it (Jas.2:10, Gal.3:10). Personal peace is fundamentally a moral spiritual problem.

Imperfect people living in an imperfect world will find stress, insecurity, anxiety, and frustration to be unavoidable. As Lily Tomlin put it, "Reality is the leading cause of stress amongst those in touch with it." It is no surprise to find Jesus commenting on stress in the Sermon on the Mount (Matt.6:25-34). He concludes the sermon with an analogy to make a point about the importance of a solid foundation for our soul as we face the stress of life in a stormy world.

Matthew 7:24-27

"24 Therefore everyone who hears these words of Mine, and acts upon them, may be compared to a wise man, who built his house upon the rock. 25 And the rain descended, and the floods came, and the winds blew, and burst against that house; and yet it did not fall, for it had been founded upon the rock. 26 And everyone who hears these words of Mine, and does not act upon them, will be like a foolish man, who built his house upon the sand. 27 And the rain descended, and the floods came, and the winds blew, and burst against that house; and it fell, and great was its fall."

Both the wise and foolish builders have an interest in and make an investment toward the building of a house. Everyone needs a place to call home, a place to live. The issue is where and how does one build it? A house is only as sound as its foundation. If the foundation is damaged or not solid, there will eventually be problems in the structure. Jesus is not talking about a physical building but rather about the inner life of the human soul and its worldview. The analogy is to be applied to the way a person lives their life and where they place their hope. In other words how should one orient his or her life? How should one live life so as to be secure and find peace? The parable can be summarized with this chart.

Foolish Builder	*Wise Builder*
Built on the sand	Built on a rock
Fails under pressure from the environment	Stands under pressure from the environment
Fails to hear and act on the Words of Jesus	Hears and acts on the Words of Jesus

"These Words of Mine" – The Sermon on the Mount

Jesus' Sermon on the Mount provides the context for our understanding *"these words of Mine"* vs.24. As we examine Jesus' teaching (Matt.5-7), a number of observations can be made. One, Jesus' sermon is largely about obedience to the Law of Moses as expressed in the Old Testament (Matt.5:17). Jesus did not come to displace the law. Two, the issue is not faith but faithfulness (Matt.7:21). It is the *"doing of the law"* that is in view. Three, the standard that is set by Jesus is very, very high. The righteousness that is demanded is greater than that seen in the lives of the most disciplined people of Jesus' day—scribes and Pharisees (Matt.5:20). Four, the demands of the moral law extend to the inner life of the heart. It is not just outward behavior that is of concern (Matt.5:21-48). Anger and lust are moral issues just like murder and adultery. Five, the blessing of

17

God is conditioned on man's obedience to the law. If we do not forgive others, we will not be forgiven (Matt.6:15). Jesus makes it clear that perfect peace is linked to perfect holiness. If individuals seek peace and security, they simply need to live holy lives. But this presents a problem, for who among us has fulfilled the demands of the law.

Jesus' words in Matthew 7 cannot be fully appreciated apart from other statements by Jesus. One, "*I have come for sinners not for the righteous*" (Matt.9:13). This statement is not meant to suggest there are some people who are not sinners, but rather there are some people who are not hungering and thirsting for righteousness they do not have. Jesus came for those who knew they needed a savior. Two, "*Blessed are those who hunger and thirst for righteousness*" (Matt.5:6). These words provide a framework for the Sermon on the Mount, and I believe reveal that the object of the sermon is to create that hunger. Three, "*I will give you rest . . . My yoke is easy and my burden is light*" (Matt.11:28-30). The moral demands of the Law of Moses (as Jesus expressed them) were certainly not easy. It is only when we are yoked to Jesus who fulfills the law, can we find its demands light. Four, the story of the Prodigal Son in Luke 15 gives hope to broken sinners not disciplined disciples. There is a fifth passage by the apostle Paul that must be kept in mind as we read Jesus' words in Matthew 7—"*the law has become our tutor to lead us to Christ, so that we may be justified by faith.*" (Gal.3:24-25). Living under the law should wet our appetite for what Christ accomplished for us in his sacrifice.

Many of us have heard the words of the children's song, "Jesus loves me this I know, for the Bible tells me so. Little ones to him belong. They are weak but he is strong." If those lines were written to express the *true* feelings of many people, they would read something like this: "Jesus loves me this I doubt, for my sins he has found out. Perfect ones to him belong, not the weak, just the strong."

Who can or has lived a perfectly pure life? The fact is only one person (Christ) has ever lived that life. The good news of the Christian Gospel is that only one person ever had to live a perfect life. The righteousness of that one man is imputed to all who are united with him by faith. But you will note that Jesus does not spell this out in the Sermon on the Mount. We know of this "righteousness of faith" because we have read the rest of the story. The Sermon on the Mount is but the appetizer for the meal that is to come. If we read Jesus carefully, we do not find immediate hope or rest. What we find is an appetite for holiness but not an aptitude for it. This is vital to our response to the Gospel of grace, which comes through the Cross of Christ. We must die before we can find life.

Basic to our understanding of peace is the foundation of holiness. A respect for and commitment to holiness sets us on the path to experience and express the peace that is in Christ. Jesus notes, *"The lamp of the body is the eye, so then if your eye is clear, your whole body will be full of light."* (Matt.6:22). If we don't see our need, we are blind.

The primary challenges to legal peace, psychological peace, and social peace are spiritual and moral. Being made in the image of God we are designed to be holy, but we are in fact sinners. The law of God reflects God's image, and it reminds us that we have not and cannot reflect the holy nature of God perfectly. That is not to say that moral laws are the problem. As Paul makes clear in Romans seven—indwelling sin is the problem not the rules. To understand the peace that comes with the Gospel message, we must read it against the backdrop of the high moral demands of the law, which require fulfillment.

It would be a grave mistake to ignore Jesus' teaching in the Sermon on the Mount. But it would be even more tragic to fail to see our inability to fulfill its demands and more tragic still to stop reading the story of the unfolding drama of redemption with the Sermon on the

Mount. The full story of the good news is yet to come through the teaching of Paul as he unpacks the meaning and power of the Word of the Cross. At this point we want to outline the profile of a wise and foolish builder. The point to be made is this: Peace is a spiritual problem that cannot be divorced from our felt need for a level of holiness that is beyond our natural ability to meet.

Acting on the Word

The Apostle Paul understood that the Old Testament Law of Moses, which Jesus expounded in the Sermon on the Mount, was able to "*give the wisdom that leads to salvation through faith which is in Christ Jesus*" (2 Tim.3:15). But how does it do this? It is significant that Paul sees the law not as a means of righteousness so much as a tool to bring insight leading to salvation. When Jesus challenges his audience to act on his words, he realizes that there is no wisdom to be gained until we see our spiritual impotence before the high standards of God's law. To simply hear his words and not seek to live them out will miss the point. It is only in our commitment to keep the law that we come face to face with our inability, which drives us to hunger and thirst for the righteousness we need. Acting on Jesus' words means that we 1) face our moral neediness, 2) develop an ear to hear the Gospel of grace, and 3) embrace the good news of Christ's death and resurrection for us. This is the wisdom that leads to salvation.

A Foolish Builder has Shallow Holiness.

Our understanding of the Sermon on the Mount is aided by the parable of the Prodigal Son (Lk.15:11-31). The older brother in the parable works hard to obey the father but is never broken to see his need for repentance. The Prodigal Son, on the other hand, is broken in spirit before his father and ultimately enjoys the blessing of fellowship with the father while the self-disciplined, proud, and bitter older brother is self-excluded from that fellowship. In this parable Jesus is speaking to people who pride themselves in keeping the law of God but fail to be broken by the high and holy demands of that law. The Sermon on the Mount

was challenging all who heard it, like the prodigal son, to find in them a broken sinner in need of grace. The foolish builder does not take the law seriously enough to experience the condemning effect it has on those under it.

A Wise Builder hungers for Perfect Holiness.

The Apostle Paul illustrates the spirit of a wise builder in Romans 7:9-10 "*I was once alive apart from the Law; but when the commandment came, sin became alive and I died; and this commandment, which was to result in life, proved to result in death for me;*" In Romans seven Paul explains the intent and affect of the demands of the law of God on his life. The law was to be taken seriously as a path to life, but it would in fact leave its well-intended disciples defeated, frustrated, and looking for the righteousness it demanded outside their personal experience. As Paul would explain, the law would lead its frustrated disciples to Christ and his righteousness, which would be accessed through faith. This righteousness would be provided *for* the believer by faith not *through* the believer by personal obedience to the law. The fact that the Holy Spirit would enable the believer to express faith through love in keeping with the law is not denied. This fruit of the Spirit is not what justifies a person before God. It is a natural byproduct of justifying faith.

Jesus is the Foundation's Cornerstone.

The Apostle Paul uses the same motif of a wise and foolish builder in 1 Corinthians 3:10-15. In this passage the foundation is "*Jesus Christ*" (vs.11) upon which the builder can build with "*gold, silver, precious stones*", or "*wood, hay, straw*" (vs.12). The quality of the building materials will determine the "reward or loss" (vs.13-15) for the builder. For our purposes in understanding Matthew seven we can simply note that the foundation for a wise builder is not only the framework of moral holiness expressed by

21

Jesus in his role as an ethics teacher but also the framework of moral holiness expressed in Jesus' role as a surrogate. He is the rock *"corner stone"* upon which the church is built

(Eph.2:20, 1 Pet.2:6-8). Before we move to the lessons conveyed through these two builders, let's see to what extent we might be Wise or Foolish. In each of the choices below circle (a) or (b), whichever you find to be most accurate:

1.
(a) The key to inner peace has to do with ridding ourselves of external moral demands.
(b) The key to inner peace is to fully embrace the high moral demands of Scripture and to find in Christ the righteousness that they demand.

2.
(a) The teaching of the Sermon on the Mount is the "end game" for living a life of inner peace.
(b) The Sermon on the Mount should be understood in the context of the Law of Moses that drives us to faith in Christ who is our righteousness.

3.
(a) A wise person is able and responsible to avoid all personal moral failure.
(b) A wise person is able to respond to personal failure with insight and faith.

4.
(a) A wise person is a person who is able to manage life through faithful obedience to Jesus' moral teaching.
(b) A wise person is a person who acknowledges the high moral demands of God and realizes that he or she cannot meet those demands.

NOTE:

The (a) statements represent a popular but inadequate understanding of wisdom.

Chapter 1
The Wise Builder

Step #1 to Peace with God:
A Spirit of Holiness

*Subjection to the full weight of God's holy law is the
foundation of the Gospel message.*

Paul as the wise builder opens his letters with the words,
"Grace" and *"Peace"*. These words express a profound
truth. The order is significant—first, grace and then, peace.
Until a person knows the grace of God (as the means), the
peace of God (as the ends) cannot be experienced. But
before a person can know grace, they must experience the
alienation from God and others that is spiritual death. The
dark background of sin and death provide a frame for the
Gospel of light (grace and peace). The core of Jesus'
ethical message was the Law of Moses that served to
expose our sin problem. He constantly reminded his
listeners of their need for holiness and reconciliation with
God. In our search for peace we must start with this same
reminder. Until we acknowledge the basic human
dilemma—a lack of holiness, we cannot appreciate the
grace of God in Christ and the peace that follows.

Don't forget chapter 3.

The first two chapters of Genesis lay a foundation for
understanding the basic order and purpose of human life.
We might say that they dignify man in his responsibility *to*
God on the one hand and his responsibility *for* the rest of
creation on the other. But it is chapter three in Genesis that
really sets the stage for the rest of the Biblical revelation as
well as the human story throughout history. Genesis three is
the account of the fall of Adam and Eve with its tragic
consequence to all creation and especially humans. We are
all "under sin" as the result of the events in Genesis 3. All
that follows—the giving of the Law of Moses, the struggle

of Israel, the coming of Christ, and the formation of the Christian church—is a response to chapter 3. We might say that the pain and suffering, the confusion and despair, and the longings and investments of modern man are to be understood in the context of chapter 3. Jesus' Sermon on the Mount is a call to remember chapter 3. The death and resurrection of Jesus is addressing the challenge of chapter 3. Our personal search for peace is to be understood in the light of chapter 3. And the two builders mentioned in Matthew 7 are distinguished by their views of chapter 3.

The wise builder avoids two mistakes. First, he refuses to divorce his life from chapter 3 and its demand for holiness. The foolish builder ignores chapter 3. The wise builder also avoids a second mistake, which is to seek reconciliation with God through the keeping of the law (experiential holiness). The law forced him to face the crippling effects of chapter 3 which extend to his inability to save himself by his own merit. On the other hand, the foolish builder feels capable of saving himself.

The Wise Builder Understands the Gospel through the lens of the Epistles.

Wise builders understand the distinct messages of both the Biblical testaments. The O.T. calls us to the Law of Moses as the path to peace. The Holy Spirit is given in the N.T. to remind us that the law is a path leading us to Christ who fulfills the demands of the law for us. This provision is the good news. It must be made clear that the power to fulfill the law resides not with us but with Christ, and the insight that leads to peace is not centered on our performance but his. The Holy Spirit is not given so we can successfully live under the law, but so that we can understand and embrace by faith the mystery of life in Christ, who fulfilled the law for us. The Holy Spirit empowers us to do good works, but this empowerment is not for the purpose of justifying us before God. Remember, the Spirit is a *paraclete* (helper, teacher, comforter) not a *surrogate* (substitute). We must not confuse the work of the Son with that of the Spirit. The good news is not about a newfound power to meet the demands of the law but rather about faith in one who has done so for us. No human can, has, or will live a life that is perfect before a holy God. But then remember, no human has to because Christ has done so for us.

When I read Jesus' Sermon on the Mount, I do not hear grace but duty. Jesus' sermon is very much like the message of the law. I am not suggesting that the theme of grace is not present in the Old Testament or the Gospels, but rather that the emphasis on the theme of grace in Paul's letters presents a dramatic contrast with much of the Old Testament and the Sermon on the Mount. Paul explains why there is this different emphasis between the period before the cross and after the death and resurrection of Christ. Paul's letters, especially Romans and Galatians, speak of a radical break between law and grace that is associated with the changing of covenants (see Section II). Paul's letters explain the relationship of the Old Covenant with the New. The Old Testament prepares us for the Gospels. The Gospels reveal the critical events of the good news of Jesus' life and death. The Epistles explain the meaning of the critical events of Jesus' life—his death and resurrection.

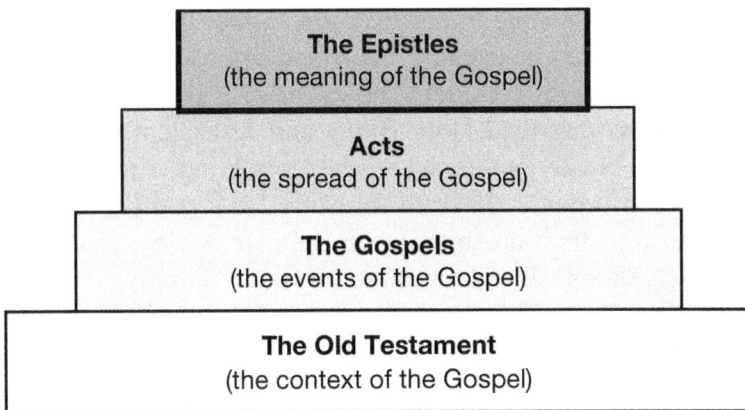

The Epistles
(the meaning of the Gospel)

Acts
(the spread of the Gospel)

The Gospels
(the events of the Gospel)

The Old Testament
(the context of the Gospel)

The Epistles are obsessed with Jesus, but the attention is focused on the meaning of the death and resurrection of

Jesus not his life and teaching. The good news of the gospel is not preoccupied with his three dramatic years of ministry but rather with the climactic end of his earthly life—his death and resurrection. When I look to the Old Testament or the Synoptic Gospels for an exposition of the "good news," I often come away with more questions than answers. I will never forget an assignment I was given while a seminary student. My professor asked our class to design a gospel tract using verses from the Synoptic Gospels (Matthew, Mark, and Luke) exclusively. As hard as we tried, we could not find texts from Matthew, Mark, and Luke that clearly explained the gospel message, as we know it today. We realized that we needed Paul's letters to complete the message.

The Wise Builder Embraces Positional Holiness.

Without holiness no one will see God, for He is holy. But in what sense can anyone ever be holy enough to match God's perfect character? We all fall short. In the Greek language the words translated "saint," "sanctified," and "holy" all come from the same root word. It means, "set apart." In the Biblical context the terms mean "set apart to God for a purpose." We usually think of holiness in the context of moral behavior where a person is said to live a holy life or someone thinks they are "holier than thou." But these words can be used of things and places that have little to do with moral conduct. The cover of a Bible may have gold letters that read Holy Bible, and Jerusalem is known as The Holy City and Israel is The Holy Land. These things are sacred because they are set aside for a godly function, not because they are morally upright. It is clear that God did not choose Israel because she was morally virtuous (Deut.9:4-7), and yet God said, *"you are a holy people to the Lord your God"* (Deut.7:6-8).

In the Old Testament a priest was required to go through a ceremonial washing (Ex.30:17-21) to be symbolically cleansed in preparation for his service in the temple. Law and tradition spelled out this ceremonial act. If it was observed properly, the priest could be assured that his service would be acceptable to God and the people. If he were not properly sanctified, he would be condemned. We might call this sanctifying procedure "positional sanctification" because it had to do with the position the priest occupied not his personal character or performance before the moral law. In other words, there were two ways a priest could be described as holy. First, he could be properly ordained in a ceremonial washing. Second, he also could be described as holy because he lived a morally upright life. Most priests were holy men in character as well as in their position. But it was possible for a priest to be "positionally" holy (counted worthy to enter the temple) while not of good character in his personal moral behavior.

Christians are described as priests, and we have been sanctified in a positional sense because of our baptism, which was a washing that set those who believe apart to serve Christ. This ceremonial washing renders us qualified to function in the presence of God without fear. Baptismal sanctification should, but does not always, result in behavioral sanctification. A Christian's conduct, which may or may not be sinless, is not the issue in acceptability before God, where we are imputed with Christ's righteousness. This is why Paul could call the Corinthian believers "*saints*" (1 Cor.1:2) and also refer to them as "*mere men*" of the world (1 Cor.3:1–4). They were positionally holy but behaviorally worldly. This will help us understand how Peter could say, "*Baptism now saves us ... through a good conscience*" (1 Pet.3:21). Our baptism into the Christian faith is not just a call to self-denial in living for God. It is also a call to find our hope and righteousness in Christ and not ourselves. "*But by His doing you are in Christ Jesus, who became to us wisdom from God, and righteousness and sanctification, and redemption.*" (1 Cor.1:30).

A point to ponder

Take your baptism seriously
knowing that God does.

The Wise Builder Embraces Imputed Righteousness.

To understand radical grace it is helpful to distinguish between four kinds of righteousness. First, there is the absolute righteousness of God set before us in nature, the Mosaic Law, and Christ. This is the perfect character of God. Second, there is the self-righteousness of people. It comes through a superficial conformity to the law of God. It is relative and may look good but in reality is incomplete. Isaiah describes this type of righteousness as "filthy rags." Third, there is the righteousness that is credited to our account apart from our behavior. We call this an imputed righteousness of faith, which is *for* us in Christ. And lastly, there is the imparted righteousness of the faithful through the power of the Holy Spirit. This is the righteousness of Christ that is lived out in the everyday walk of obedient Christians. It is the life that people can see—the fruit of imputed righteousness.

Four Kinds of Righteousness

Absolute	*Self*	*Imputed*	*Imparted*
Perfect	Phony	Perfect	Partial
God's nature	Of my human effort	Of Christ through faith	Of the Spirit through growth
Of God alone	Of all people	To all Christians	For all who obey Christ

Paul's words are shocking in Romans 4:5 where he writes of *"Him who justifies the ungodly."* God actually declares as "just" the one who is in practice "ungodly." We must distinguish between our "passive righteousness" which is imputed *to* us by faith, and "active righteousness" which is lived out *through* us by the power of the Spirit.

Imputed not imparted righteousness is the "righteousness of faith." Paul writes of these two types of righteousness in nearly all of his letters. Romans, like most of Paul's letters, can be divided into two sections. In chapters 1–11 we read of the righteousness of God *for* us—the imputed righteousness of faith. This is the great indicative of who we are in Christ. In chapters 12–16 we read of the righteousness of God *through* us—the imparted righteousness of the Spirit empowering us to obey. This is the great imperative. The order is important—first the imputed righteousness, then the imparted righteousness.

Romans

Chapters 1–11	*Chapters 12–16*
The righteousness of God for us	The righteousness of God through us
The indicative: our identity in Christ	The imperative: our conduct as Christians
Imputed righteousness Justification	Imparted righteousness Sanctification

In the same way and to the same extent that Christ who was sinless took our sins, we who are sinners took his righteousness. Jesus became a sinner for us. We who are "in Christ" are as righteous as Christ. If we can believe that Christ took our sins, we can believe that we take his righteousness. "He made Him who knew no sin to be sin on our behalf, so that we might become the righteousness of God in Him." (2 Cor.5:21). Three great imputations underlie the biblical gospel. There is the imputation of Adam's sin to the human race. There is the imputation of the sins of the world to Christ and also an imputation of the righteousness of Christ to all who believe in him.

In the same way and to the same extent that Christ who was sinless took our sins, we who are sinners took his righteousness. Jesus became a sinner for us. We who are "in Christ" are as righteous as Christ. If we can believe that Christ took our sins, we should be able to believe that we take his righteousness. "He made Him who knew no sin to be sin on our behalf, so that we might become the righteousness of God in Him." (2 Cor.5:21). Three great imputations underlie the biblical gospel. There is the imputation of Adam's sin to the human race. There is the imputation of the sins of the world to Christ and also an imputation of the righteousness of Christ to all who believe in him.

Three Great Imputations

Of Adam's sin	Of man's sin	Of God's righteousness
To all who are "in Adam" by natural birth	To Christ the "second Adam" on the Cross	To all who are "in Christ" by spiritual birth

When someone occupies the office of the President of the United States, he is given the authority to speak on behalf of the country. He may not know how everyone he represents feels or thinks, but when he speaks as president, he speaks for the whole country. When we are said to be "in Adam," we share the guilt of Adam's sin even before we sin as Adam sinned (Rom.5:12,19). When we are said to be "in Christ," we share the righteousness of Christ even before we have displayed any righteous behavior.

The Wise Builder Believes Apart from Experiencing.

A distinction between the believer's position in Christ and the believer's performance as a Christian is important to understand. A positional relationship has the following characteristics:

First, it is a legal relationship. Our position in Christ is something that is declared by God to be true because of His grace received by faith. It is like the declaration of a court of law or an athletic official's call in a game. The declaration of guilt or innocence, of being "in bounds" or "out of bounds," may not reflect the actual experiential facts but it nonetheless stands as binding. Second, it is a static relationship. It does not change. It does not grow or decrease. It is not affected by how we feel, act, or think. There is no holiness hierarchy in our position in Christ. We are all seen as equal in Christ. Third, it is not an experiential relationship. We should have a deep sense of peace or renewed energy and motivation to worship and serve because of a realization of our position in Christ, but then again, we may not. This is not something that comes over us as a charismatic experience. We must receive it by faith. Fourth, it is the result of God's grace through our faith. The believer's positional relationship "in Christ" is not a reward for obedience; it is a gift of grace applied through faith. By faith I mean we must trust that this is true because we are taught that it took place. Without the assurance of Biblical revelation we would not know this truth and therefore would not believe it. This leads to the final observation. Fifth, it is learned through teaching. It is not natural, intuitive, experiential, or a social discipline. It must be learned and believed. The Apostles were called to teach this. It is the message of the church's teaching today.

Our positional relationship with God in Christ is linked to what theologians call "justification." This relationship is the result of our faith in Christ who died "for us." Because of this position we are perfect and complete "in Christ." There is no spiritual "class system" with respect to justification. Obedient Christians and disobedient Christians are on the same level in justification before God.

Our position in Christ	*Our performance in this life*
We are perfect children of God	We are growing disciples of Christ
This is the foundation of discipleship	This is the expression of sonship
This is the result of our legal adoption by Christ	This is the result of our experiential abiding in Christ
This is Christ's work for us on the cross.	This is Christ's life in & through us by the Spirit.
This is passive righteousness	This is active righteousness
This is external to us	This is internal (within us)
This is our legal position	This is our living performance
This is the result of coming to Christ	This is the result of following after Christ
"If we live by the Spirit"	"let us walk by the Spirit."
Justification	Sanctification

Luther referred to this justification as "passive righteousness." It is not dependent upon our performance. Luther believed it is on the basis of the "alien" or "extrinsic" righteousness of Christ that God justifies or declares the sinner just. This justification is not progressive but complete, total, finished, perfect even though the believer is still a sinner—*Simul Justus et peccator* (at the same time justified and a sinner).

The Wise Builder Understands the Corinthian Saints

The Apostle Paul expressed an inner peace while being outwardly stressed as a prisoner. This got my attention. His testimony so impressed me that I started a personal search to understand what he knew that I did not. In that search I encountered another testimony that would prove to be formative in my understanding of Paul's "secret." It was Paul's letter to the Corinthians where he addresses these sinning Corinthian Christians as holy— "*saints by calling.*"

The Corinthians were acting like non-believers yet were called "saints." Paul called them "*saints*" (from the word "sanctified") when he said: "*to the church of God which is at Corinth, to those who have been sanctified in Christ Jesus, saints by calling, with all who in every place call upon the name of our Lord Jesus Christ, their Lord and ours*" (1 Cor.1:2). Later in the same letter, after pointing out the sins of the worldly Corinthians, he says, "*And such were some of you; but you were washed, but you were sanctified, but you were justified in the name of the Lord Jesus Christ, and in the Spirit of our God*" (1 Cor.6:11). Clearly some of the believers in Corinth were not faithful, for they were still acting like non-believers (1 Cor.3:1). Why did Paul say they "*were*" (past tense) sinners when in fact they still sinned? The answer is found in the way Paul says these same people "*were*" sanctified, "*by faith in Christ*" (apart from their present behavior). Justification has to do with one's faith identity in Christ. A person is a Christian because of personal faith in the sufficiency of Christ. Christians live out their new identity as they express their justification.

The Wise Builder Sees the Good News as a "Good Shepherd" rather than as "good sheep."

"Sanctification" is the word theologians use to describe the "imparted righteousness" of the Spirit. Many Christians confuse justification and sanctification, faith and faithfulness. This confusion leads to the belief that God's grace justifies a person by empowering the believer to live a righteous life through the enabling of the Holy Spirit. Some believe that the "new birth" (a clean heart) produces fruit (a good life), and that the "good life" justifies a person before God. In this view there can be no absolute assurance of salvation until the final judgment because we will never know until then if we have been good enough long enough. In 1542 Pope Paul III convoked a council that rejected (by a vote of 32 to 5) the Reformer's doctrine of justification by faith alone in favor of a transformationist view of justification, where justification is but the first step in sanctification (salvation). To this day, Protestants and Roman Catholics are distinguished by this difference. The Protestant reformation was based upon an understanding of justification as "a declaration of righteousness," not a "making righteous in character." The righteousness of faith is a righteousness that is imputed to our lives, not implemented in and through our lives. At the cross Jesus had no sin but yours and mine. And at the judgment we have no righteousness but His. In making this radical statement I am not suggesting that holy living is unimportant, or that it should be of little concern to us. It is very important, but it is not the issue with respect to our justification and our legal (perfect) peace with God.

A point to ponder

To the extent and in the same way
that Christ bore our sins,
we bear his righteousness.

Questions for Discussion

1. What are some of the dangers in confusing our position in Christ with our performance?

2. Is there also a danger in isolating our justification by faith from our sanctification in this life?

3. Are there parts of this chapter with which you disagree? Why?

Chapter 2
The Foolish Builder or Unbroken Sinner

Obstacle #1 to Peace with God: A Lawless Spirit

Our hunger for peace is fueled by our shame.

If we understand the full demands of a holy God we will be humbled, broken, and frustrated with our lives. What we may not realize is that we also may be among the wise builders. A fool does not take Jesus' words seriously but rather edits them to make their moral demands manageable. A fool is not broken before God. Our frustration before the law brings us to the foot of the cross and to the water of life in Christ. That is where we all should be and it is only there that we will find peace.

A graduate student friend grew up in a foreign country not hearing the gospel message until he studied in the U.S. Many of his graduate school colleagues rejected the Gospel dismissing the Bible and the historicity of Jesus' resurrection. They started with the question, "Can I trust the biblical message to be true?" They concluded they could not and moved on.

My friend however started with a very different question: "Where is there forgiveness for what I know to be painfully true about me—my guilt and shame? I do not know if the Bible is true, but I do know that my soul is hungry for release from the prison of shame." Indeed, this is a common question that people ask no matter what their intellectual concerns may be. We all sense there is something not right in the world, and the problem extends to our own soul's shame. Most of us feel the tinge of guilt, no matter what our religious tradition. What my friend aptly identified was the need for personal forgiveness and peace. At the core of our longings we find a restless soul and an emptiness that only God can fill.

There are two great dissonances in the lives of most people. One source of anxiety is cognitive or intellectual. It strives to reconcile the many conflicting and paradoxical messages that bombard our inquiring minds. The other is a moral dissonance—the painful gap between what we ought to do and what we actually do. At the end of the day I find the moral dissonance to be more pressing than our intellectual questions.

We must start with what we personally know to be true, the simple fact that we have frustrated longings for justice, peace, and wholeness. We are disappointed with others and with our environment, since they seem to repeatedly block or sabotage our efforts to drink deeply of our vision for a true, rich, and full life. But even more frustrating is our disappointment with ourselves. Far too often we have been guilty of the very thing we despise in others. We want and need others to stop looking out only for their own interests and start loving us as they should. But in our very demand for love we expose the ugly fact that we act with the same selfishness we condemn in others. Our most pressing questions are not intellectual but moral not social but personal. When we first acknowledge and address the truth of our shame and guilt, we will then be better able to address the issue of the truthfulness of the biblical revelation. Where do we find an answer to the dilemma of our culpability in the pain of the universe? Where do we find rest and peace for our souls?

When my friend encountered the biblical story of God's gracious forgiveness through Christ, his heart leaped for joy; and he began a search to see if God's promise could be true. With an "ear to hear" he satisfied his mind that the Christ of the Gospels was one to whom he could trust his life. He approached the Bible with an open heart and mind wanting to believe that its message was true. His "ear to hear" made all the difference in how he engaged the legitimate intellectual questions needing to be answered. St Augustine put it like this: "Faith is to believe what we do not see, and the reward of this faith is to see what we believe." Anselm added: "I do not seek to understand that I may believe, but I believe in order to understand."

The Foolish Builder does not feel the Weight of Holiness.

Who is the fool who builds his house on the sand (Matt.7:26)? He is the one who does not take Jesus' words in the Sermon on the Mount seriously and does not feel the weight of the law's demands on fallen sinners. He is the person who seeks peace with God, self, and the world by lowering the bar of the law's demands so they can be managed. The Sermon on the Mount is laced with references to the misguided assumptions of the religious leaders of Jesus' day—*"You have heard that . . ."* (Matt.5:21, 27, 31, 33, 38, 43), *"Unless your righteousness surpasses that of the scribes and Pharisees"* (Matt.5:20), *"Beware of practicing your righteousness before men"* (Matt.6:1), *"Beware of the false prophets"* (Matt.7:15). When facing the high moral demands of the law, we can do one of three things. We can extend the time that we have to meet those demands—purgatory. We can lower the bar— redefining the law so we can manage its demands. Or we can fall on our knees and hunger and thirst for a righteousness that we need, do not have, and cannot achieve. It is the lowering of the bar that Jesus is challenging in his sermon. Paul expresses this well in Romans 7:7-25 where he says the law brought death to him not life.

The Foolish Builder does not see that the Yoke of Jesus is light.

As Jesus' disciples faced the greatest crisis of their lives— his death, Jesus offered them a peace that the world could not. *"Peace I leave with you: My peace I give to you: not as the world gives do I give to you. Let not your heart be troubled nor let it be fearful"* (Jn.14:27). But does not the world offer us peace? The answer depends on what kind of peace we are talking about. There are many paths that promise rest for the soul, and we experience peace on different levels. A house built on sand may stand for a while and function well for a season, but over time its vulnerability will be exposed and it will fall. The house built on sand is the life that has rendered the demands of a holy God manageable apart from Christ ("law-lite" pp 73).

Jesus said, *"Come to me, all who are weary and heavy laden, and I will give you rest. Take my yoke upon you, and learn from Me, for I am gentle and humble in heart, and you shall find rest for your souls. For My yoke is easy, and My load is light."* (Matt.11:28–30) To be yoked with Jesus means that he pulls for and with us. Our role is easy when he does the work. He pulls and we share the benefits. The yoke is the law, and we are yoked to Jesus, the only one who can fulfill it. Because we are yoked with him, we share the benefits of his work.

Inner peace comes not from holiness of our own but from Christ's holiness. It is not for those who are content to live outside the demands of the moral law but for those who are crushed by it as they are forced to realize that they need a redeemer. It is for those who long for a peace that the world cannot give or take away. The first step to finding that peace is the realization of our own inadequacy in solving the problem. This is the subtle but powerful point of the Sermon on the Mount and this is the critical point that the foolish builder does not get.

The Foolish Builder does not see that the Root of Social Peace is Legal Peace.

The Apostle Paul writes his letter to Philippians from prison at a time when his circumstances could hardly be described as pleasant. He was called by God to bring the Gospel to the Gentiles and here he sits "out of commission" with respect to the Roman Empire, forsaken by other Christians, cold and alone. But when we read his letters from prison, we find his heart is full of gratitude and grace. He demonstrated a peace that freed him from the terror of a hostile world while at the same time being fully engaged with that world. But it is not just Paul's outward circumstances that were a challenge to his peace. In Romans seven he describes himself as a wretched man who did not do what he knew he should and was shamed by his sinful nature before the demands of the law. Yet he can say in Romans 7:25-8:1 *"Thanks be to God through Jesus Christ our Lord! . . . there is now no condemnation for those who are in Christ Jesus"* The gospel of grace freed him from the frustrating struggle with keeping the moral law even as he strove to obey God and follow Christ.

Christ offers us three spheres of peace. There is first a *legal* peace with God that comes from being pardoned from sin through the sacrifice of Christ. Second, the *psychological* experience of peace comes from sensing God loves us unconditionally in Christ. Third, *social* peace comes from living a gracious life in community with others. The first has to do with what Christ did *for* us, the second with what he does *in* us, and the third with what he does *through* us. Paul captures the idea in 2 Corinthians 13:14 *"The grace of the Lord Jesus Christ, and the love of God, and the fellowship of the Holy Spirit, be with you all."*

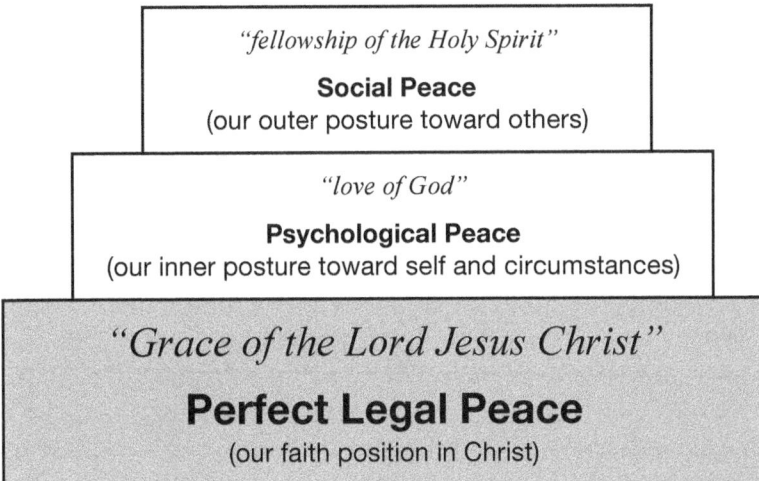

"fellowship of the Holy Spirit"
Social Peace
(our outer posture toward others)

"love of God"
Psychological Peace
(our inner posture toward self and circumstances)

"Grace of the Lord Jesus Christ"
Perfect Legal Peace
(our faith position in Christ)

Peace starts with the legal reconciliation between God and those who are in Christ by faith. This peace is perfect and it renders the sinner holy. It cannot be improved upon or diminished. It is our position in Christ. It is the foundation for both psychological peace and social peace. It is a peace that equips a person to endure and even thrive in a hostile environment of misunderstanding, abuse, injustice, and neglect at the hands of man and nature. It is not the kind of peace that is dependent upon personal moral merit, nor is it diminished by personal moral failure. It is a peace that enabled a man like the Apostle Paul to write a letter of joy from prison. It is a peace that enabled a woman like Sarah to trust herself to God in a dysfunctional marriage. It is a peace that enabled a man like Steven to face an untimely death with dignity and confidence. It is a peace that enables Mary to worship at the feet of Jesus even when there is work to be done. It is a peace that enables a gracious master to forgive a large debt and absorb the loss. It is a peace that enabled Jesus to sense God's love even as he is called to bear the sins of the world and the torture of the cross. It is the object of the Cross of Christ. It is the essence of the Old Testament's *Shalom*. It is the object of the New Testament's Gospel. The foolish builder misses all of this as he is set on a path leading to inner and outer conflict.

The Foolish Builder does not know Strategic Peace.

We experience a certain measure of peace when we get a financial raise, or have a favorable doctor's report, or see our children succeed. The experience of peace that comes at these good times in our lives is real and enjoyable but fleeting and superficial. A deeper sense of peace comes from satisfying relationships with one's family and friends. When we are successful in our work and given an opportunity to use our creativity and talents to help society, we experience a sense of peace that is not superficial. This peace is associated with inner fulfillment. But the kinds of peace I have described thus far share one thing in common: they depend on circumstances that may or may not happen;

if they do happen, they may not last. The world gives and takes away. This is "tactical (temporal, superficial) peace."

We want and need a more strategic (abiding, deep, overarching peace, the kind that enables Paul to write an epistle of joy from prison. Tactical peace is tied to our environment and our performance. Strategic peace is the rest within our souls that enables us to face the complexities of life, painful circumstances, even our own failures, and the failures of others with grace and a gentle spirit. It is this strategic peace that enables us to experience rest in our souls when the conditions for tactical peace are not present, or when we sense that they may not be coming. One of the really critical phenomenons of Strategic Peace is that it works not through but in spite of the circumstances that govern tactical peace. It is a peace that is remarkably immune to the fickle experiences in this world.

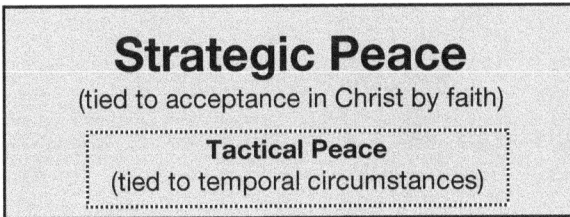

Strategic Peace
(tied to acceptance in Christ by faith)

Tactical Peace
(tied to temporal circumstances)

Have you ever been surprised by people who had everything going for them in this world (fame, fortune, etc.) and yet seemed to still lack psychological or social peace? They may be depressed, divorced, and on drugs in a continued search to find something beyond the fame and fortune, which did not satisfy the deepest itch in their souls. By way of contrast, I have a relationship with three inmates at a local prison who are serving long sentences. I have never sensed anything but gratitude from them for the way in which their incarceration has led to spiritual renewal. Prison life is not comfortable, and when a person is there because of some injustice in the legal system, it is even harder to endure. In this context a display of strategic peace is powerful. The joy and peace I sense from these guys has nothing to do with their outer circumstances. It has everything to do with their Christian faith.

When I was deep in financial debt as a student, I felt that life's worries and troubles would be over once I had a savings account. Later I discovered that when I was out of debt and had fewer financial worries, life was still full of anxieties. The deep relief that I expected was not experienced. Being free from debt provided only superficial peace as I came to realize my soul's restlessness was deeper than financial anxiety. You may feel if you just had a better marriage, better health, better job, better education, better something, all would be well with your soul. It might be temporarily better to find tactical peace with such blessings, but I maintain the strategic peace that your soul seeks will not be found in anything this world has to offer. Any attempt to satisfy the core longings of the human soul through imperfect people in an imperfect world will be like the house built on the sand.

Are You Wise or Foolish?

What effect does the law as expressed by the "Sermon on the Mount" have on you? Does it give you comfort and assurance, or does it break you leaving you searching for salvation from its condemnation? Does it set your face toward the Gospel story so that the imputed righteousness of Christ by faith is truly good news? A wise person takes seriously the full demands of the law and is broken by them. The foolish person does not allow the full force of the law to break his or her soul. Or more often, the foolish person waters down the force of the law's demands so that they can be managed through Christian discipline. It is hard to imagine the Sermon on the Mount as good news unless it leads us to the cross of Christ.

Chapter 3
God's Peace Plan

Grace and Peace are the essence of the Gospel.

A Parable of Grace

A wealthy man had three sons who were bound for college, but each son had no money to enter the elite school they had chosen to attend. To the first son the father said, "I will give you a job to earn money so you can one day pay for your education." To the second son he said, "I will loan you enough money to go to college, but if you fail to make good grades or drop out, you will be expected to pay me back all I have loaned you." To the third son he said, "I will give you enough money to go to college with the expectation you will finish with good grades—but even if you do not meet my expectations, the money is a free gift to you." Now which of the three son's experiences illustrates the grace of the father? The answer is that each of the stories illustrates the father's grace but in different ways and to different extents.

Which of these three son's experiences best illustrates the Christian Gospel? The first son's experience is not unlike the posture of the legalist whereby God enabled him (by grace) to earn his way to eternal life. We might say in this case the Gospel is "front end loaded" with the requirement of moral virtue. The second son's experience can be likened to those who "back end load" the Gospel with the requirement of obedience. The grace of God in this case is conditioned upon the performance of the person *after* he is justified. If the believer fails to be obedient, he does not ratify his eternal life or lose it. The third son's experience can be likened to radical grace where the gift is unconditional. It is expected that the believer will be obedient and meet the demands of the Kingdom, but even if he does not, he still retains the gift of eternal life.

This analogy frames a debate that continues within the Christian community today. There is general agreement among Protestants that the experience of the first son does not represent the Gospel. But there is not a clear agreement as to which of the other two sons best illustrates the true Gospel. Is the gift of eternal life conditioned on the faithfulness of the recipient? Is true faith marked by faithfulness? A more detailed discussion of this debate can be found in the second book in this series *Peace Makers,* but for now we will let Paul speak.

Which Gospel?

Jesus came proclaiming the Gospel of the Kingdom inviting all to *"repent and believe the Gospel."* What was he expecting folks to believe? Was it the Gospel that Paul defined in 1 Corinthians 15:1-5 centered in the Cross and Resurrection of Jesus? The cross and resurrection were unknown until the end of Jesus' earthly ministry, and their full significance were not made clear until after Pentecost. How are we, today, to understand the relationship between the Gospel OF Jesus' Cross and Resurrection preached by Paul and the Gospel preached BY Jesus which centered on the Kingdom? Was Jesus' Gospel a message to the nation Israel only? Did it embody the hope that Israel would be restored to its place of blessing after years of captivity? Was the restoration to be social and political as well as spiritual? Was Israel to be equated with the church (the Body of Christ) or limited to the nation? This issue is complex and controversial. I cannot do it justice in this book but I mention it to clarify a point of tension with respect to the Gospels and the Epistles.

The Gospel preached BY Jesus was clarified, explained, and superseded by the Gospel OF Jesus' Cross and Resurrection preached by the Apostles. If we define the Christian message of "good news" only or primarily from the Gospel of the Kingdom preached by Jesus, we will at least be confused if not misled in that it must be understood in the context of the Old Covenant. The following chart points out some of the contrasts between the Gospel BY Christ and the Gospel OF Christ.

The Gospel BY Christ	The Gospel OF Christ
Preached by Christ	Preached by the Apostles
Centered on the Kingdom	Centered on the Cross
Called for repentance from sins against the law	Called for repentance from dead works
Focused on obedience	Focused on faith
Proclaimed BEFORE Pentecost in the four Gospels	Proclaimed AFTER Pentecost in Acts and the Epistles
The emphasis is on obedience to the law	The emphasis is on the reception of grace
Is preached in the context of the OLD COVENANT	Is preached in the context of the NEW COVENANT

Paul's Gospel of Grace leads to Works.

How did Paul understand the relationship between faith and obedience, between belief and behavior? To answer this question we go to Romans chapter eight where Paul begins, *"There is therefore now no condemnation for those who are in Christ Jesus"* (vs.1). In verses 2–3 Paul summarizes what he explained in chapters three through five: *"For the law of the Spirit of life in Christ Jesus has set you free from the law of sin and of death. For what the law could not do, weak as it was through the flesh, God did sending his own Son in the likeness of sinful flesh and as an offering for sin, He condemned sin in the flesh."* Here Paul states that the requirements of the law WERE (past tense) fulfilled FOR us (we could not do it) in Christ.

In verse 4 Paul goes on to explain that this freedom from condemnation is to bear fruit in our inner lives. It satisfies the demands of the law in us—*"in order that the requirement of the Law might be fulfilled in us, who do not walk according to the flesh, but according to the Spirit."*

45

The fruit of the law is fulfilled in us (peace) as we experience our union with Christ through faith, as we walk in the Spirit, that is, as we set our minds on our identity "in Christ." (Rom.8:5–7). The believer and nonbeliever are distinguished by this spiritual paradigm shift—changed "mindset" or way of looking at themselves.

It also can be said that as we cooperate with the Spirit of Christ in us, the love that is demanded by the law is fulfilled through us (sanctification). We are recognized as Christians by our love, which is the "end result"—the behavioral objective of the law and the fruit of the Spirit.

This same message is repeated in Ephesians 2:8–9, *"For by grace you have been saved through faith; and that not of yourselves, it is the gift of God; not as a result of works, that no one should boast."* Again, we see Christ's work *for* us followed by verse ten where we read of Christ's work *in* and *through* us. *"For we are his workmanship, created in Christ Jesus for good works, which God prepared beforehand, that we should walk in them."*

A point to ponder

God's work for us is
the basis of and followed by
His work in and through us.

This pattern of legal justification leading to Godly living is seen often in Paul's writings. For example, Ephesians 5:8 says, *"For you were formerly darkness, but now you are light in the Lord; walk as children of light (for the fruit of the light consists in all goodness and righteousness and truth),"* and Galatians 5:25 says, *"If we live by the Spirit, let us also walk by the Spirit."*

Going back to Romans chapter eight, we see this pattern developing in Paul's argument as he traces the path between faith and obedience. The believer is first reconciled to God (vs.1–2), then regenerated in Spirit (vs.3–4), and finally renewed in mind (vs.5–13).

In Romans 8:5–8 Paul talks of two mindsets: *"For those who are according to the flesh set their minds on the things of the flesh, but those who are according to the Spirit, the things of the Spirit. For the mind set on the flesh is death, but the mind set on the Spirit is life and peace,"* There are two ways we can look at ourselves as Christians. We can see ourselves as we are in the flesh. This is the view that the law demands of us, a view that measures us by our deeds meaning we will be condemned; for we all fall short in one way or another. In chapter seven Paul gives his own testimony of how painful it was to live under the law captive to the flesh and its flaws.

However there is another way that Christians can see themselves. They can set their minds on "the Spirit", that is to say, "the new nature of the believer." In this sense, the believer is free from the condemnation of the law and is holy, justified, and perfect in Christ. From this perspective, the believer has peace with God. These two ways of looking at oneself explain why Paul could so quickly and dramatically switch from the *"wretched man"* of Romans 7:24 to the *"thanks be to God"* man of 7:25.

Lest there be any confusion about the believer's identity, Paul reminds us that we are indeed *"in the Spirit,"* no longer "in the flesh." Romans 8:9–10 reads, *"However, you are not in the flesh but in the Spirit, if indeed the Spirit of God dwells in you. But if anyone does not have the Spirit of Christ, he does not belong to Him. And if Christ is in you, though the body is dead because of sin, yet the spirit is alive because of righteousness. But if the Spirit of Him who raised Jesus from the dead dwells in you, He who raised Christ Jesus from the dead will also give life to your mortal bodies through his Spirit who indwells you."* This static position that we have in Christ must be distinguished from the dynamic posture that we have in our day-to-day walk. One is perfect; the other is in process.

Paul makes it clear that obedience is expected but not automatic or inevitable for the believer. In verses 12–13 he exhorts us, *"So then, brethren, we are under obligation, not to the flesh, to live according to the flesh—for if you are living according to the flesh, you must die; but if by the Spirit you are putting to death the deeds of the body, you will live."* The Greek word translated *"under obligation"* is the word for *"debtor"*. We are indebted to the new self in Christ because our new life is a gift to us. Walking in the power of the Spirit is not a requirement that notarizes our faith. Justification before God is not conditioned upon the Spirit's work through us. It is a mindset, an understanding of union with Christ that draws us to Christ's likeness.

A point to ponder

The Gospel is about a Good Shepherd not about good sheep.

Now we can summarize the message of Romans 8:1–13. First, to walk in the Spirit I must first know that I am secure in Christ through new birth (Rom.8:1–2). Second, I must expect to live as a disciple of Christ through my new life in Christ (Rom.8:3–4). This process will cultivate a way of seeing my life in the Spirit through a renewed mind (Rom.8:5–13). To be renewed in my mind I must respect the importance of the mind in spiritual warfare. I must also reason together with God concerning my new, true identity and replace the impulses of the flesh with those of the Spirit.

It wasn't until I read Romans 6 and Philippians 3 that I began to understand Paul's teaching on grace. In Romans 6 Paul talks about dying with Christ to the old life and rising with Christ to a new life. But in my real life experience I did not feel or act dead to my old life. When I looked at Philippians 3, however, I saw that I was not alone in my experience. Paul too was not yet dead and raised in his EXPERIENCE. He was in process, *"pressing on,"* but with thankfulness and joy in his struggles. This is the crux of faith versus obedience. Victory, peace, and joy in Christ are not primarily freedom from all sinful behavior but freedom from condemnation of the law, because we are positionally sanctified in Christ. Christ is our peace. We see him as much more than an instrumental means of power enabling us to obey the law so as to acquire peace. Radical grace links God's blessing to simple but sincere faith in Christ with no accounting of personal performance, either by human effort or divine enablement before or after coming to Christ. The devil offers peace through anything and everything but Christ. God presents a peace that the world can't give or take away. What separates us from God is not our sin so much as our damnable "good works"—our commitment to be worthy of justification before God IN OURSELVES (Heb.6:1).

Common Fallacies

There are three common fallacies in our view of God's grace. The first fallacy is that God's grace is relative. Some folks wrongly believe God is gracious—forgiving and accepting—only to those who generally try harder, do better, and believe more sincerely than the average person. Their thinking goes like this: God is not unreasonable. He knows no one is perfect, but the good people are distinct enough from the bad to justify God's vindication or wrath on the really bad ones. For example, Adolph Hitler should not expect to receive God's grace while Mother Theresa should expect it. Why? In the case of Mother Theresa it is because her life is relatively good. And in the case of Adolph Hitler it is because his life is relatively bad.

The Roman Catholic tradition has provided a doctrine of purgatory to extend the time in which true holiness can be achieved. In this life trying hard, confessing failures, and regular observation of the Mass will do. But if we have not fully attained to the standard of our "new life in Christ" by the time we die, we have a place where we can be brought up to standard after death—purgatory. As I said earlier, the Roman Catholic Church addresses the problem by extending the time; some Protestant churches address the problem of human frailty by lowering the bar. According to this view if we are sincere, try hard, confess our sins, and get the needed help to repent of "big sins," we can feel secure and be at peace. Both systems miss the point of the nature of God's grace in Christ, which frees us from the condemnation of the law covenant with its focus on MY works. It is no longer about me. It is all about Jesus.

A point to ponder

God grades on the Cross
not on the curve.

A second false view of God's grace (a more refined version of the first) is that true faith equals obedience to the law. Although no one is perfect, Christians who are filled with the Spirit and walking by faith can subject themselves to the law and fulfill it—sort of. This view holds that God forgives and accepts those who truly trust and as a result faithfully follow Christ. Those who hold this view remind us that God saves by grace through faith alone, but faith that saves is never alone. They also remind us that you can identify the saved by their works. So in the final analysis it is the fruit that counts according to this view. Some who hold this view will be very quick to defend justification by faith apart from works, but in the day-to-day dynamics of one's relationship with God, obedience to the law is viewed as the test. The blessings and punishments of this life are viewed as signs of God's love or rejection based upon one's obedience to the rules.

A third false view of God's grace defines God's basic nature as gracious, and sees everyone as forgiven apart from what they might believe or do. In other words if we start with a gracious God, we then must understand everything else—such as moral law and holiness—in the context of grace. This is the logic of "universalism"—everyone is justified no matter what they believe or do.

I've often tried my hand at crafting a definition of God's grace. My first attempt went something like this: "Grace is the blessing of God given apart from moral merit." Reduced to a simple phrase it would be "unmerited favor." But the more I thought about it, the more I was troubled by that definition. As I studied Paul, I have come to realize grace can only be understood in the context of moral merit or law. For grace is never free. It is linked to moral merit but not our merit. It is the moral merit of Jesus that makes God's grace available to the believer. The just demands of the holy character of God can be met either *by* us or *for* us, but they must be met. The life and death of Christ make the blessing due God's Son available to us through faith as Paul tells us in Romans 3:25–26, *"Whom God displayed publicly as a propitiation in His blood through faith. This was to demonstrate His righteousness, because in the forbearance of God He passed over the sins previously committed; for the demonstration, I say, of His righteousness at the present time, that He might be just and the justifier of the one who has faith in Jesus."*

So then grace is best understood in the context of God's holiness and moral law, not apart from it. Grace is the imputation of moral virtue apart from moral performance. No wonder Paul had such high regard for the law. He proclaimed—not its illegitimacy—but our liberation from its just condemnation. This means we are imputed with the righteousness of Christ by faith. *"He who knew no sin became sin for us that we might become the righteousness of God in him"* (2 Cor.5:21). This imputation is apart from our own performance as Paul declares in

51

Romans 4:4–5, *"Now to the one who works, his wage is not reckoned as a favor but as what is due. But to the one who does not work, but believes in Him who justifies the ungodly, his faith is reckoned as righteousness."*

> **A point to ponder**
>
> God justifies not the righteous
> but the ungodly by faith.

There are many questions that probably arise at this point. What is true faith? What about all those biblical texts that seem to contradict the idea of radical grace? The following chapters expound on answers to these and other vital questions. The Appendix at the end of this book offers a response to several texts that seem to challenge the Gospel of grace. But first let me offer a series of test questions that are designed to highlight some of the most misunderstood issues with respect to God's grace. In each of the following ten choices, circle (a) or (b), whichever you believe to be most accurate:

1.
(a) God gives a person right standing with Him by making that person an innocent and virtuous disciple.
(b) God gives a person right standing with Him by mercifully accounting that person innocent and virtuous.

2.
(a) God gives a person right standing with Him by crediting a person with Christ's goodness and virtue.

(b) God justifies a person by putting Christ's goodness and virtue into the person's heart resulting in the person becoming Christ-like from the inside out.

3.
(a) If a Christian becomes "born again" (regenerated, transformed in character), he or she will achieve right standing with God.

(b) If the sinner accepts right standing with God by faith, he or she will experience a change in character.

4.

(a) Victory over sin is defined by our faith and confidence in Christ's work for and through us.

(b) Victory over sin is defined by our actual performance of the demands of the law.

5.

(a) We achieve right standing with God by having Christ live out His life of obedience in us.

(b) We achieve right standing with God by accepting the fact that He obeyed the law perfectly for us.

6.

(a) We follow Christ's example because His life has given us right standing with God.

(b) We achieve right standing with God by following Christ's example with the help of His enabling Spirit.

7.

(a) God sends His Spirit to make us good, and then He will pronounce we are justified.

(b) God first pronounces we are good in His sight, and then gives us His Spirit to make us good.

8.

(a) God is glorified when we trust fully in Christ even when we are not perfectly obedient.

(b) God is glorified only when we obey his holy law by the power of the Spirit.

9.

(a) By the power of the Holy Spirit living in us, we can fully satisfy the claims of the Ten Commandments.

(b) Only by faith in the perfect life and atoning death of Christ can we fully satisfy the claims of the Ten Commandments.

NOTE:

The (b) statements in even numbers and (a) in the odd numbers represent a misunderstanding of God's grace.

Steps of Application

1. Test yourself with the questions and statements above. To what extent do you understand grace in this radical way?

2. Identify the specific areas of your life where guilt has been or is present. In prayer turn each area over to God as an opportunity for Him to reveal His grace to you.

3. Keep a journal of specific areas of your life where grace has replaced shame and guilt.

4. Note your behavior and attitude in relationships with others and in responses to circumstances. How do you feel and what do you think about your performance? Make needed changes.

Questions for Discussion

1. What is your story with respect to law and grace, shame and peace, and being declared righteous and acting righteously?

2. Does this radical understanding of grace make you nervous? Why?

3. How do you resolve the tension between law and grace in Scripture?

4. How do people sense God's radical grace?

5. Are there parts of this chapter with which you disagree? Why?

Section II

Grace and Law

The Story of Two Mothers: Sarah and Hagar

*Grace frees us from the law covenant
demanding we perfectly fulfill
the standards of a holy God.*

Christian congregations and denominations can be divided into two groups—HOLINESS churches and GRACE churches. The holiness churches uphold the moral law of God and the wrath of God. These churches and their people tend to be against everything that gets close to looking like sins of the flesh—fornication, drunkenness, "worldly" amusements, etc. They are separatist as they seek to protect themselves from defilement by the world. There are lots of rules to obey, spiritual police to enforce the rules, and dire consequences for all who disobey them. The grace churches make a different impression. They have a much more relaxed attitude toward those who struggle with moral imperfection. The sermons and policies in these churches emphasize love expressed in tolerance and mercy. These congregations are willing to eagerly accept the folks who are kicked out of the holiness churches. The people in these churches seem comfortable mixing it up with the broader culture and welcoming open dialogue with those who disagree with them. Needless to say there is considerable tension between these two groups. The holiness people tend to look at the grace churches as lukewarm and worldly. The grace churches tend to feel sorry for the holiness groups criticizing their legalism and preoccupation with moral superficiality, separatism, and fear.

The distinction between holiness and grace people is more than a matter of style or temperament. It is often deeply embedded in their respective theological understanding and faith. We will explore this theological divide in Galatians 4:21–31 as we look at the story of two mothers—Sarah and Hagar.

A House Divided

Someone once asked, "Where in the Bible does it teach man cannot have two wives?" Maybe in Matthew 6:24 where it reads: "*Man cannot serve two masters.*" We are going to look at a story from Genesis that is interpreted for us in Galatians. It is about two women in one household. Both served a purpose, but ultimately the house was not big enough for two. The reason one was kicked out provides a spiritual allegory that is the basis of perhaps the greatest theological watershed in all Christendom and is a key to correctly discerning the Gospel message.

The great philosopher/theologian Jonathan Edwards said, "There is perhaps no part of divinity attended with so much intricacy, and wherein orthodox divines do so much differ as stating the precise agreement and difference between the two dispensations of Moses and Christ." He recognized the tension between the law of the Old Testament and the grace of the New. These two systems have a profound effect on our understanding of the Gospel.

While grace is a theme found throughout the entire Bible, it is expressed most powerfully in Paul's writings where he explains the significance of Christ's death and resurrection as it applies to our sinful condition. Paul's letter to the Galatians presents a compelling case for radical grace. In this section we are going to see how God has used the law covenant through Moses to first teach us about our sin problem and then lead us to Christ, who brings us out from under the curse of the law. While the Law of Moses continues to provide a moral guide to believers, its tutorial and condemning function is not aimed primarily at Christians but rather at those who have not yet come to see their need for Christ.

To appreciate Paul's teaching in Galatians, we must first visit the book of Genesis where we find a story that Paul will use as an allegory in his exposition of the tension between law and grace. The story in Genesis 16–21 is one of the great family dramas of the Bible. The narrative is framed in the context of a promise made to a man by the name of Abram. God promises Abram a son through whom the world would be blessed. Yet Sarah, Abram's wife, is barren, so she convinces Abram to use her Egyptian maid, Hagar, as a means to produce the promised son. Tension between Sarah and Hagar is inevitable, and when Hagar conceives, it explodes to the surface. Sarah seeks Abram's help in dealing with her rival, Hagar. Abram grants Sarah permission to deal with Hagar as she sees fit. The conflict intensifies resulting in Hagar spending much of her time fleeing from Sarah. God's care for Hagar in her distress is a hint at the important role she will play in God's overarching plan. Hagar is instructed by God to return to Sarah where she bears a son, Ishmael, who is prophesied to be the source of a great nation (the Arab people)—a generation that will live at odds with the descendents of Sarah's offspring (the sons of Israel).

When we move ahead to chapter 21 of Genesis, we find that eventually Sarah births her own son, Isaac. When Isaac is weaned, Hagar's son, Ishmael, mocks him; and Sarah demands that Hagar and her son be banished. Abram complies, and Hagar is cast out to live on her own. Again God encourages Hagar and cares for her even though it is clear God's plan will be worked out through Isaac.

One cannot help but be impressed with the efforts of Sarah and Abram to see the purposes of God fulfilled through them. The problem comes with the involvement of Hagar, which supplants the work of the Spirit. In Paul's recounting the story in his letter to the Galatians he picks up the tension between flesh and spirit. His purpose is to use the story to explain and resolve the dissonance between the Old and New Covenants.

Galatians 4:21–31 (NIV)

"21 Tell me, you who want to be under the Law, are you not aware of what the Law says? 22 For it is written that Abraham had two sons, one by the slave woman and the other by the free woman. 23 His son by the slave woman was born in the ordinary way; but his son by the free woman was born as the result of a promise. 24 These things may be taken figuratively, for the women represent two covenants.

One covenant is from Mount Sinai and bears children who are to be slaves: This is Hagar. 25 Now Hagar stands for Mount Sinai in Arabia and corresponds to the present city of Jerusalem, because she is in slavery with her children. 26 But the Jerusalem that is above is free, and she is our mother. 27 For it is written

> "Be glad, O barren woman,
> who bears no children;
> break forth and cry aloud,
> you who have no labor pains;
> because more are the children
> of the desolate woman
> than of her who has a husband."

28 Now you, brothers, like Isaac, are children of promise. 29 At that time the son born in the ordinary way persecuted the son born by the power of the Spirit. It is the same now. 30 But what does the Scripture say? "Get rid of the slave woman and her son, for the slave woman's son will never share in the inheritance with the free woman's son." 31 Therefore, brothers, we are not children of the slave woman, but of the free woman."

Paul begins this passage by asking a question: "*Do you who want to be under the Law (that is, to measure your standing before God on the basis of your faithfulness to the commandments), not listen to the Law?*" In other words, "Don't you understand how the law is presented in the larger scope of God's plan?" The law will do nothing but condemn you. It should not be something you want to live under, if you expect to find peace with God.

God's plan for the redemption of His people begins to take shape with a promise given to Abraham for a special son. One son, Ishmael, was by his concubine Hagar. This son was of "*the flesh,*" that is, the fruit of Abraham's own plan and effort. The other son, Isaac, was by his aging wife Sarah. This son was "*of the promise,*" a son born by a miracle of God (given Sarah's old age) and in keeping with God's promised plan to bless the world.

Paul is using a common first century Hebrew interpretive technique called *midrash* (taking a text from one context and applying it to a very different context in keeping with the present need of the interpreter). Paul tells us these mothers in the Genesis narrative represent two covenants (vs.24–28). Hagar was the covenant of law given at Mt. Sinai to Israel through Moses and represented the Jewish religion. Sarah was the covenant of grace in Christ and represented Christianity. The first mother, Hagar, is cast out, being incompatible with the promise given to Abraham that was fulfilled in the second mother Sarah.

Grace is pictured as freedom in contrast to the bondage of the law. Hagar is called the "*bondwoman,*" while Sarah is called the "*free woman.*" Paul tells us the law covenant represented by the Old Testament creates a family of slaves, while the grace covenant in Christ creates children who are free from the guilt and pride associated with the law. The sons of the bondwoman were historically at odds with the sons of the free woman. So too the children of the law (Judaizers) persecute the children of grace (Christians). The point of the story, however, comes in Galatians 4:30–31, *"But what does the Scripture say? 'Cast out the bondwoman and her son, for the son of the bond-woman shall not be an heir with the son of the free woman.' So then, brethren, we are not children of a bondwoman, but of the free woman."* The two mothers were not to coexist. The two covenants cannot coexist either. This is the point: law and grace are mutually exclusive as covenants.

In upcoming chapters we will examine Sarah and Hagar as representatives of two systems: law and grace. We will first look at Sarah and learn what it means to live a life under the radical grace of the New Covenant. Following Sarah's life we will discover peace is ours when we walk in freedom from the condemnation of the law, having died to it in Christ. We will then look at Hagar to discover the proper and improper use of the law realizing that before we can experience God's peace, we must let the moral law 1) crush our human attempts to be righteous by our own effort, and 2) lead us to faith in Christ who will be our righteousness. In the process we will address the Christian's relationship to the law. How can the law be used lawfully? What constitutes a "Pharisee spirit?" Are we able and expected to perfectly obey the law with the power of the Spirit? In what sense are believers free from the law?

Hagar	*Sarah*
Children of the flesh	Children of the promise
The covenant at Sinai (Law)	The covenant at Calvary (Grace)
Bondwoman	Free woman
Judaizers	Christians
Hagar (the old covenant) is cast out	Sarah (the new covenant) remains

Before we move to the lessons conveyed through these two mothers, let's see to what extent we might be a spiritual child of Hagar or Sarah. In each of the choices below circle (a) or (b), whichever you find to be most accurate:

1.

(a) The biggest problem in the modern church is a lack of moral discipline.

(b) The greatest problem in the modern church is a lack of thankfulness and faith in God.

2.

(a) The greatest need in my life is more faith to trust God and walk in the knowledge that He really loves me.

(b) The greatest need in my life is more power to live a life that overcomes sin.

3.

(a) Even when I sin, I do not feel condemned by God but rather sorrow and disappointment with myself.

(b) I often feel condemned and guilty, even when I am not sure if I have done something wrong.

4.

(a) I know when I have done wrong, but I don't obsess about it; nor do I keep score of the misdeeds of others.

(b) I tend to keep score of my own behavior as well as the moral behavior of those around me, and I keep kicking myself for messing up.

5.

(a) God has more love for me when I live a sacrificially holy life.

(b) God's love for me is total because I am "in Christ," and I bring more joy to Him when I seek Him and live a life of worship.

6.

(a) I have a hard time worshiping, because I would much rather get teaching and help in overcoming some of my bad habits.

(b) I delight in worship and find my spirit renewed as I am reminded of God's grace.

7.

(a) Grace makes me sensitive to sin and even more sensitive to repentance and worship.

(b) Grace means I can live my life without ever having to say to God or anyone I am sorry.

8.

(a) Because I am not under the law, I give little attention to the Ten Commandments because they do not apply to me.

(b) Because I am fully accepted in Christ, I want to know all I can about Him and His will for me.

9.

(a) I have a hard time forgiving myself when I sin.

(b) I can move past my failures with thankfulness for God's grace and a desire to learn from my experience.

10.

(a) I am afraid sooner or later God's patience will run out with my failure to manage life according to His rules.

(b) I feel very secure in my relationship with God even though I know I am not perfect.

11.

(a) My greatest passion is to know Christ and make him known to others through my life.

(b) My greatest passion is to have total victory over sin so I won't feel any shame.

12.

(a) I have a hard time with preachers who always talk about grace and don't balance it with law.

(b) I need to hear the message of grace over and over in ways that challenge me to worship, obey, and serve.

NOTE:

The (a) statements represent a popular but inadequate understanding of God's law in all but #2,3,4,7,11 where it is just the reverse.

Chapter 4
Sarah – It's Her House Now

Step #2 to Peace with God:
A New Covenant Spirit

*To experience peace with God we must
walk in the freedom of the New Covenant,
having died to the law.*

There is a saying in Chapel Hill, NC that the only person to hold the legendary basketball star Michael Jordan to below 20 points in a game was Dean Smith, his college coach. When MJ started to play professionally, he averaged over 30 points per game. Why did he not do that in college? Very simple, it was not a part of coach Smith's law or style of play and game plan. What if Dean Smith phoned MJ while playing in the NBA and said, "You can't do this or that because that's not the way we play at Carolina." MJ might listen, but he would have no compulsion to obey his old coach because he was no longer at Carolina. With a new contract under a new coach and a new system there are new expectations and different rules. The wisdom learned while at UNC under Smith's system was not forgotten or rejected. Much of it was internalized and expressed dramatically in the NBA. In the spiritual realm we have been redeemed or transferred from one system and are now living under another. We have learned much from living under the law but are now free from it as a master.

We who live under the New Covenant as children of Sarah have a calling that is higher, deeper, and truer to God's nature than the law given to Moses. Jesus is our new clear standard and revelation of holiness. In Jesus we see a perfect blend of grace and truth. Grace is evident because the condemnation demanded by the Old Covenant is absorbed in the Cross of Christ. Truth reveals itself in the fullness of the Godhead manifested most clearly in Jesus' ministry. We might liken the New Covenant to a new operating system installed in a computer to replace an old system. The old and new systems share a lot of similarities but are nonetheless independent of one another. The following key points guide us through the new system.

The New System is Internal not External.

The covenant Jesus introduced at the Last Supper (Lk.22:20) takes on a fresh significance in light of the New Covenant spoken of in Jeremiah 31:31–34 *"I will put My law within them and on their heart I will write it. . . . for they will all know me."* It is contrasted with the Old Covenant when the prophet says, *"Not . . . like the covenant I made with their forefathers"* (Jer.31:32). The Old Covenant was largely an external (superficial) expression. The New Covenant operated more from within the heart. The New Covenant is an inside – out system. In John's Gospel Jesus prepares his disciples for the New Covenant blessing with these words, *"He* (the Spirit) *abides with you and will be in you."* 14:17 and *"He will teach you all things."* 14:26. When the Holy Spirit was given at Pentecost, Jeremiah's prophecy was fulfilled. The New Covenant enlightened God's people and generated a number of blessings like:

1) *a deep personal relationship with Christ.* Disciples would not just know about an untouchable God. They would know God as though they were one with Him.

2) *an instinctive response to God.* They would not have to always look for a Scripture passage, counselor, or special revelation to know God's will. Godliness would now be a part of their nature as the Spirit guided them.

3) *an integrated life.* They would have a level of integrity as never before. They would be sons of God not slaves.

4) *an insight into the Gospel.* They would "get it" in the sense that the things that were confusing concerning Jesus would now become clear. The word of the Cross would be seen as the power and wisdom of God (1 Cor.1:23-24).

Hagar and Sarah's story explains the special relationship of these two redemptive covenants. The following chart identifies some of the distinctive characteristics of the Old and New Covenants.

SINAI	CALVARY
Operates from the outside - in	Operates from the inside - out
Through Moses	Through Christ
Israel is the focus	The Church is the focus
Law	Grace
Conditioned upon man's obedience	Conditioned upon Christ's obedience
Based upon works	Based upon faith
Was concluded at the cross	Was initiated at the cross
Earthly, sinful high priests	Heavenly, sinless high priest
Earthly tabernacle	True (heavenly) tabernacle
Faulty	Faultless
Limited access to God	Free access to God
An anxious conscience	A cleansed conscience
Demanded obedience	Enabled obedience
Exodus – Gospels	Acts – Revelation

The New Covenant Christ introduced was not an "upgrade" of the Old Covenant Moses introduced, but it was a new system linked to the promise given to Abraham; a system based on grace, not human merit; a system received by faith, not works; a system that operated from the inside – out, not externally. Now, to be sure, the Old Covenant was a part of God's gracious plan to deliver on His promise to Abraham. It was a necessary step preparing us to recognize and respond to Christ. As John reminds us in John 1:17, *"For the Law was given through Moses;*

grace and truth were realized through Jesus Christ." If we are to comprehend radical grace and experience the peace it offers, we must appreciate the above distinctions. But we also need to see the New Covenant in the context of the Promise given to Abraham.

The New Covenant has a distinct relationship with the Promise and the Law.

The Old Covenant was temporary in nature and was an appeal to the flesh to obey the law. It was to produce guilt in the face of inevitable human failure as opposed to comfort and assurance through human discipline (Rom.7:5–13). As such it was not the end but a means to appreciate a better covenant. In John 1:17 the Old Covenant was contrasted with the grace of the promise to Abraham fulfilled at the cross. The law was a temporary tutor until Christ, when it was dissolved (Gal.3:19–25). The New Covenant in Christ would fulfill the Promise of Abraham.

The Promise given to Abraham (400 years before Moses) – unilateral and unconditional	
Step #1: *The Old Covenant* (15th century BC)	**Step #2:** *The New Covenant* (1st century AD)
The Law of Moses was a tutorial preparing us for the promise by showing us our problem and God's provision.	The cross and resurrection of Christ was a fulfillment of the promise to redeem and make holy through faith in Christ.
Terminated at the cross	Inaugurated at the cross
Circumcision required	No more Circumcision

The Cross of Christ is the
Final Chapter in the Old System.

Like any contract the Old Covenant had terms that were to be fulfilled. The law required payment for sins committed, and the sacrificial system of the Old Covenant offered a temporary stopgap payment for transgressions. This payment had to be renewed yearly. With the once-for-all sacrifice of Christ, complete satisfaction for sin was accomplished (Heb.10:1–18). The fulfillment and termination of the law covenant is what Paul has in mind when he talks about being redeemed *"from under the law"* in Galatians 4:5 and 1 Corinthians 9:20. In Galatians 5:1–6 Paul exhorts believers with these words, *"It was for freedom that Christ set us free; therefore keep standing firm and do not be subject again to a yoke of slavery. Behold I, Paul, say to you that if you receive circumcision, Christ will be of no benefit to you. And I testify again to every man who receives circumcision, that he is under obligation to keep the whole Law."*

Circumcision was a sign of the Old Covenant, and while very important to those living under the law Covenant, it was not appropriate once that covenant had been terminated. In 1 Corinthians 6:12 Paul testifies *"all things are lawful for me, but not all things are profitable. All things are lawful for me, but I will not be mastered by anything."* Paul indicates he is constrained by his new nature in Christ but not by the Law of Moses in that he is "not under law." He looks to something other than the law for security.

It was Christ who removed believers out from under the law covenant in Paul's understanding. Consider his statements in Galatians 4:21–31, *"Tell me, you who want to be under Law, do you not listen to the Law? – So then, brethren, we are not children of a bondwoman, but of the free woman."* In Galatians 5:18 we read, *"But if you are led by the Spirit, you are not under the Law."* and in

Romans 6:14, *"For sin shall not be master over you, for you are not under law, but under grace."*

Christians Die to the Old System in their Baptism.

While the law was to convict sinners of their need for faith in Christ, the goal was not to continue to hold in bondage those who had come to faith in Christ. Nor did the law provide a path to victory through the power of the Spirit working in us to obey its demands. Bondage to sin through the law was broken by death not moral discipline. Believers who died with Christ through their baptism (union) with Christ also died to the power of the law to condemn. We are first set free by the Cross and then renewed in this life by the Spirit.

Paul talks about believers being dead to the law as a means of achieving righteousness through their faith in Romans 7:1,4,6: *"The Law has jurisdiction over a person as long as he lives ... You were made to die to the Law through the body of Christ ... But now we have been released from the Law, having died to that by which we were bound."* Note also 10:4: *"For Christ is the end of the Law for righteousness to everyone who believes."* Galatians 2:19 also makes this point: *"For through the Law I died to the Law, that I might live to God."*

It is important for us to be very clear in stating that the law which was terminated as a covenant included not just the ceremonial commands but also the moral proscriptions. When Paul talks about the law, he has the Mount Sinai Commandments in mind. For example, in Galatians 4:21–31 we read, *"One covenant is from Mount Sinai and bears children who are to be slaves: This is Hagar. . . . Therefore, brothers, we are not children of the slave woman, but of the free woman."* In Colossians 2:14, he talks about Christ *"having canceled out the certificate of debt consisting of decrees against us and which was hostile to us; and he has taken it out of the way, having nailed it to the cross."* And in 2 Corinthians 3:11 he says, *"For if that which fades away (vs.7 "the ministry of death, in letters engraved on stones") was with glory, much more that which remains is in glory."*

In Romans 7:1–12 Paul uses a powerful illustration of marriage to make his point. A widow is freed from the marriage covenant after her husband's death. In the same way we died with Christ to the law covenant and therefore cannot be judged under that law. First, the principle is stated in verse one, *"Or do you not know, brethren (for I am speaking to those who know the law), that the law has jurisdiction over a person as long as he lives?"* Paul next applies an analogy to demonstrate what he means (vs.2–3), *"For the married woman is bound by law to her husband while he is living; but if her husband dies, she is released from the law concerning the husband. So then if, while her husband is living, she is joined to another man, she shall be called an adulteress; but if her husband dies, she is free from the Law, so that she is not an adulteress, though she is joined to another man."* Note here that the rightness or wrongness of the woman's actions is not in her behavior per say but in the law that is in force at the time of her behavior. Her behavior is adulterous while the law of marriage is alive through her first husband. When she is freed from that law, her (same) behavior is no longer counted as adultery. Paul describes our death to the law as liberation from its power to condemn us for behavior, which during the law's rule would have rightly brought condemnation. In verses 4–6 he applies the principle of the believer's death with Christ, *"Therefore, my brethren, you also were made to die to the Law through the body of Christ, that you might be joined to another, to Him who was raised from the dead, that we might bear fruit for God. For while we were in the flesh, the sinful passions, which were {aroused} by the Law, were at work in the members of our body to bear fruit for death. But now we have been released from the Law, having died to that by which we were bound, so that we serve in newness of the Spirit and not in oldness of the letter."*

Paul recognizes that his readers may wrongly conclude that the law is not of God and therefore something to be despised. He rejects this conclusion by explaining that the law is not the problem, rather our sin, which is aggravated by the law. *"What shall we say then? Is the Law sin? May it never be! On the contrary, I would not have come to know sin except through the Law; for I would not have known about coveting if the Law had not said, 'You shall not covet.' But sin, taking opportunity through the commandment, produced in me coveting of every kind; for apart from the Law sin {is} dead. And I was once alive apart from the Law; but when the commandment came, sin became alive, and I died; and this commandment, which was to result in life, proved to result in death for me; for sin, taking opportunity through the commandment, deceived me, and through it killed me. So then, the Law is holy, and the commandment is holy and righteous and good."* (Rom.7:8–12.)

Legal Fine Print can Nullify the New Contract.

Every contract has some fine print. Too often our message of grace is on target, but the fine print in the details may feel like law. When a church emphasizes the subject of grace in its preaching of the gospel, it does well. But if at the same time its practices are legalistic (focused on law), it sends a mixed message. I am thinking of a congregation in the Midwest that had a detailed list of rules inside the back cover of its hymnals. To be a member in good standing it was expected that you followed these rules which included—tithing, church attendance three times per week, as well as a long list of substances to avoid like tobacco, alcohol, long hair, short skirts, playing cards, dancing, and the list went on. No matter how hard the preacher might preach "grace," the fine print was a deafening "LAW." This was reinforced by the way in which "rule breakers" were discriminated against. If we preach grace, we need to get Hagar out of our lives. Law and grace stand in bold contrast to each other. Don't misunderstand me at this point. There is a need for moral standards and discipline in the Christian's life, but we must be careful to challenge disciples to obey in response to grace not in fear of condemnation that was settled at the Cross.

	Law	*Grace*
Our basic relationship with God	**Earned by our performance**	**Given because of Christ's performance**
Our daily walk with God	**Repeatedly earned by our performance**	**Given because of Christ's work and as a consequence of following Biblical teachings**
Our motivation for obedience	**External - based on fear and guilt**	**Internal - based on love and thankfulness**
Our source of power	**Our own discipline and sense of duty**	**The Holy Spirit enlightening and strengthening our renewed lives**
The results	**Condemnation**	**Salvation**

Does Grace Enable us to Fulfill the Old Contract?

Let's take a quick review. In revealing the holy nature of God, the law exposed the sinfulness of God's people (Rom.3:20, 5:20, 7:7,12,13). The law excites and inspires our efforts to be holy, but we are not able to be holy (Rom.8:3, 7:18–25; Heb.7:18). This is why the law is called a minister of death and bondage (Gal.4:3,9; 2 Cor.3:6,7,9; Rom.7:5), preparing people for the gospel of Christ (Gal.3:24). The law uncovered a moral impulse and longing that was sensed even before the law was revealed—a desire to "do good", which was written on our hearts. This longing for moral excellence was accompanied by a deep sense of failure, guilt, and shame for not living up to expectations. The law came to expose us to our true fallen nature and create a moral dissonance that would find relief in the cross of Christ. In the book of Romans Paul expresses this purpose of the law: *"And the Law came in that the transgression might increase"* (Rom.5:20), *"that every mouth may be closed, and all the world may become accountable to God because by the works of the Law no flesh will be justified in His sight; for through the Law comes the knowledge of sin"* (Rom.3:19–20). It is in this context we are to appreciate Jesus' exposition of the law in the Sermon on the Mount where He raises the moral bar by defining murder as hatred, adultery as lust, justice as mercy, and love as a gift to the enemy (Matt.5). When Jesus said He came to fulfill the law (Matt.5:17), He was indicating He would first correct the watered down interpretation of the law that the Pharisees had used to justify themselves. When Jesus got through with His exposition of the law, no one would be standing before God with a moral record they could be proud of or find confidence in. To use Paul's words, *"every mouth would be closed."*

The first step to recovery for many alcoholics is "hitting the bottom of the barrel." Until a person is so despairing of their own inability that they have no fight left, they will seldom take the steps needed for recovery. One of the tragedies for many alcoholics comes with well meaning friends and family who try to keep the alcoholic from crashing. The loving motivation to help a person escape the pain of the gutter can enable the alcoholic to manage the problem without ever addressing or solving it. The same is true of the law. Sometimes we are taught we can and should be able to manage our lives under the law. We become little Pharisees if we are successful, or "spiritual failures" if we are not. But either way we don't come to the end of self and as a result to the grace of God in Christ.

Churches too often serve up what I refer to as "law-lite." Law-lite is a watered down form of the law that can be managed with human discipline and a little whitewashing here and there. Law-lite will not tolerate drunkenness with wine, while it views pride, bitterness, and envy as only human. It will not tolerate murder, but anger may be overlooked. Under "law-lite" we might not feel condemned, but we may feel proud. The fact that God resists the proud and gives mercy to the condemned should unsettle us. There is a certain peace that comes from living successfully under "law-lite," but it is not the peace of God. The Pharisee of Jesus' day had adopted a "law-lite" position that was manageable through human discipline. The Sermon on the Mount (Matt.5–7) represented Jesus' response to this problem of watering down the just demands of a holy God with man-made standards and traditions.

The true law of God	*"law-lite"*
Is rooted in the holy nature of God	Is rooted in the traditions of man
Cannot be perfectly obeyed by mortal mankind—only by Christ	Can be managed by mankind with discipline
Leads to condemnation, Christ, and faith	Leads to pride, manipulation, fear, and the work of the flesh
Is not the measure of a Christian's relationship with God and is not fulfilled except by Christ	Can be successfully followed and is believed to establish the believer before God
Is radical in its definition of sin, demanding complete perfection	Is selective in what it chooses to define as mortal sin

Love is a Better Motivation than Law.

One of the great misconceptions of radical grace is that it does not take sin seriously enough. It is not that grace ignores sin but rather that grace has a special way of responding to it. The argument Paul used in confronting sin in the early church was not threat of condemnation or promise of material reward, but rather an appeal to one's identity as a new creation in Christ (Rom.6).

I have often wondered why some children rebel after growing up in strict Christian homes where right and wrong values are clearly taught and consequences for wrong conduct are strictly enforced? I have sensed that in many cases the rebellion has been an escape from a family culture that was better at motivating with fear and shame than with grace and love. When I asked our own children for insight into the troubled relationships of some of their friends, they responded with comments like, "Their folks are too unreasonable and strict." "They don't feel like their parents are really concerned about understanding them." Such comments suggested to me that speaking the truth in love was not taking place in some of the homes. It is hard to rebel against those whom we sense really love us and take the time to understand us. I can never remember doubting my parent's love as I grew up. They may not have always done the right thing, but I always sensed they had the right heart. Maybe this is why my two brothers and I never really had to rebel in order to become independent. It is hard to turn away from love. Sadly in both the social and the spiritual realms some people can rebel and for a time turn away from love, but this is unnatural.

Sarah is a spiritual mother who leads her children in the path of freedom. We must realize this freedom is both an entitlement and a test. We can abuse it or honor God with it. God takes a great risk when He sets us free. He counts on the power of love to keep us in check and draw us to Him as disciples. We follow Him because it is His love we want to know and share. Spiritual warfare involves resisting the temptation to live by law not love. The bonds of love are far stronger than the bonds of law. When we know God's love, we will follow God's law without fear of rejection or need of reward.

Grace can use the Law as a Moral Compass without fear of its Condemnation.

Radical grace is willing to face the full force of the law's demands and the condemnation that results from our failure. It is a mistake to assume that Jesus expects Christians to meet the challenge of the ethical standards of the Sermon on the Mount. Christians have not, do not, and will not live out the *full demands* of the law because they cannot. When dedicated, spirit-filled, and mature Christians read the Sermon on the Mount and expect to live by it perfectly so as to gain or keep God's favor, the results are disappointing, because the law is designed to convict and condemn not assure and encourage. The revelation of sin and the sense of guilt that results intentionally push us to the cross of Christ where we die with him in baptism and also die to the law's convicting authority. Grace picks up the pieces after the law has convicted and condemned.

The law is not intended to control and comfort us, although that is the way it is often used. It will only control and comfort those who look at it superficially. I regret that so many preachers who believe in the grace of God come to the portions of the Bible that teach the law and teach it as though we were under its domain. The results are too often tragic where people are confused at best and robbed of the doorway to radical grace and peace at worst. If we preach the law, let us do so as part of the good news of grace. And then move out from under its domain as a covenant of condemnation for our failure to keep its demands. Let us not go back and think we can handle *all* of its demands even with the newfound power of the Spirit. In the end the law will minister death to all who place themselves under it as a covenant. A life of grace can use the law as a moral compass, but it has no fear of its condemnation.

Grace is Seen most Clearly in the Context of Sin.

The focus of the Old Covenant (Hagar) was sin. The focus of the New Covenant (Sarah) is grace. We are children of

Hagar when we think of the Christian life primarily in terms of our moral success and failure before the law of God. We are children of Sarah when we see sin as an opportunity to move toward God's love and grace. This is not to belittle sin, for our sins are always before us; but they must be processed through the Cross.

Grace is viewed as unnecessary and insignificant when we lose contact with our own sinfulness. The law is vital to grace in that it creates a framework for grace by exposing sin as sin. We marginalize grace to the extent we downplay sin. Excusing sin in the name of liberty will mean grace loses its power and glory. To use Paul's words from Romans 5:20, *"And the Law came in that the transgression might increase; but where sin increased, grace abounded all the more."* The great joy expressed by Paul in the last verse of Romans 7, *"Thanks be to God through Jesus Christ,"* comes immediately after—and in the context of—the pain expressed in the previous verse (24), *"Wretched man that I am!"* Grace does not overlook sin but takes it most seriously. The following chart shows the path to grace and peace.

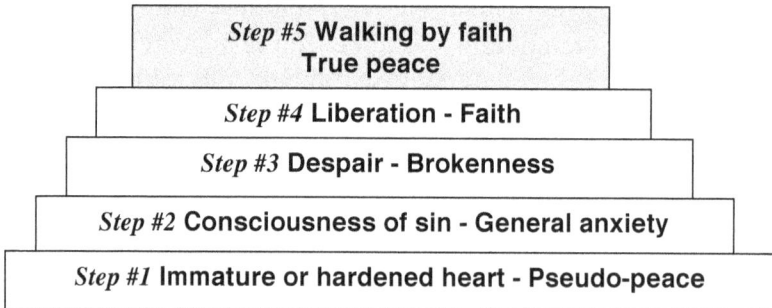

Step #5 **Walking by faith True peace**
Step #4 **Liberation - Faith**
Step #3 **Despair - Brokenness**
Step #2 **Consciousness of sin - General anxiety**
Step #1 **Immature or hardened heart - Pseudo-peace**

At step #1 a person is asleep to the moral demands of God. This can be the result of immaturity or the result of a hardness of heart, a spirit of lawlessness, and a persistent resistance to God. This condition can be difficult to correct as in the case of the sociopath personality. But sometimes it is accessible to God's Spirit and can lead to a moral awakening through exposure to the law of God.

Step #2 is characterized by a general uneasiness with self. It is the condition of sensing something is wrong, without knowing what it is exactly. This condition is often the result of repressed guilt and displays itself as depression. The help of a skilled counselor or close friend may be needed to unpack the source of the anxiety.

Step #3 is associated with a conscious awareness of sin. It is the stage where we feel shame and condemnation before God leading to brokenness. The person may feel unworthy of the name "Christian." In trying to cope with the dissonance of guilt a person can use moral discipline, rebellion, false humility, or other coping mechanisms—or they can move to the next step in true repentance and faith.

Step #4 is the point of encounter with radical grace through brokenness and repentance. It can arise through a number of means. Some discover it, as Luther did, through the study of Scripture. Some experience it as a charismatic encounter that floods them with a sense of God's love. Still others come to realize God's grace through the process of counseling. One of the most common means of realizing God's grace is the environment of a loving church or home. Perhaps the least preferred path to experiencing God's grace is via dramatic pain and failure.

Step #5 is the state of a relaxed attitude that the Bible describes as a peace that is beyond understanding. This peace is characterized by deep joy and gratitude enabling those who have it to be peacemakers among others. It is a peace that frees us to follow Christ with faith, discipline, and hope motivated by love.

People who are burdened with guilt and anxiety over sin are candidates for radical grace. It is far better to suffer the pain of being "under the law" than to live "over the law," repressing the truth of God's holiness and our shame. The spiritual sociopath (the person with a hardened heart) is at a place of arrested spiritual development and further from a vital relationship with God than a person full of shame, anxiety, and guilt. Cheap grace is not grace that is devoid of disciplined obedience but rather grace that is devoid of brokenness through a deep sense of sin and a failure to appreciate the price paid at the cross.

Grace is for Convicts, not Outlaws.

I have known individuals who championed God's grace but seemed to have no sensitivity to the holy demands of God's law. They were not under the law. They were "above the law" or outside the domain of the law. The grace of the Gospel is free from the law but not above or outside the law. People who know radical grace also know brokenness. Grace is for people who have been under the curse of the law, not for those who have no conviction before the law.

When we tame the law with our watered-down understanding of its demands, it may become more manageable through human discipline; but in the process we feel no need for deliverance and thus no appetite for Jesus' cross or Paul's doctrine of radical grace. This is why the "religious spirit" of legalism is so devastating. It keeps the law from driving us to despair by making it doable. In this sense the legalist does not suffer from having "too much" law but "not enough." He or she has not allowed the full weight of the law to crush all hope in self. Those who either ignore or manage the law will not fully appreciate their deliverer, because they don't see their imprisoned condition and their desperate need for a Savior.

Such arrogance before the law was illustrated by some of the religious folks of the first century. In John 8 Jesus speaks to religious people who were not aware of their own sin. They blindly believed they had the law under control and were managing life quite well. Jesus tells them in verse 34 that they are really slaves to sin, and as slaves the master of the house will cast them out unless the Son who is secure in the house sets them free (Jn.8:35–36). Their response was what we might expect from those not under conviction. They were insulted and unreceptive, convinced they had the state of their souls under control.

78

The freedom Jesus had in mind for these religious people would not come from a new superhuman power to carry out the law. Rather Jesus offered himself as one who could take away the curse of the law through the cross. The eighth chapter of John starts with the story of the woman caught in adultery who is pardoned by Jesus. But Jesus' pardon is not to be taken as disrespect for the demands of the Law of Moses. He spoke out of a broader perspective, not condemning her because He knew He would soon be condemned *for* her. Let it never be said that the radical grace of the gospel does not take the law seriously. It pays the ultimate respect for the law by letting its demands define the life and death of Jesus. The condemnation of the law is applied not only to my neighbor and myself, but also to Christ for He bore sin unto death as the law demanded. We must let the demands of the Law deeply convict us if we are to enter into the walk of grace. Liberation is for convicts, not outlaws.

> ### A point to ponder
>
> Christ "fulfills the demands" of the Law
> without the believer
> "doing the works" of the Law.

"Fulfilling" (not "doing") the law is a legitimate part of every Christian's testimony. "Fulfillment" has to do with the perfect satisfaction of the law's demands that comes only through a believer's identification with Christ by faith (Rom.8:4). It is a vicarious (substitutionary) fulfillment of the law by Christ, not an experiential "doing the works of the law" by us that secures our relationship with God.

The law and grace in Christ do not represent two coexisting and enduring aspects of God's covenant of redemption but rather two successive eras in salvation history that are vital to each other. The law as a tutor prepares us to appreciate and welcome Christ as Redeemer. The grace of the New Covenant sets us free from the bondage created by the law. Without the law we would not appreciate God's grace in Christ. This will be the subject of chapter six as we explore the value of the law in our lives.

Questions for Application and Discussion

1. In what ways does knowledge of legal contracts help or hinder our understanding of theological covenants?

2. What is the role of the Cross and Resurrection in marking the transition between Old and New Covenants?

3. How do baptism and the Lord's Supper give us insight into the Old and New Covenant life?

4. How do the two covenants affect the way we define and view sin?

5. How would you summarize this chapter?

6. Are there things in this chapter with which you disagree? Why?

Chapter 5
Getting Used to a New Operating System

The New Covenant will introduce some welcome features
but also call for some challenging adjustments.

A middle-aged couple joined our congregation when they moved into our town. They had been a part of a large denomination that was noted for its conservative theology and were delighted to hear and see the grace oriented culture in their new church family. But after two years they still tended to revert to their old church's way of seeing the world. They continued to struggle with shame and blame. They understood God's grace with their mind and welcomed it emotionally, but changing from one worldview to another proved to be difficult in the face of behaviors that were so deeply embedded from years of experience. The legalism of their previous congregation was more deeply engrained in their lives than they realized, and they found themselves stuck. It took years before they were set free.

There is always a learning curve with the installation of a new system on a computer. We have to learn some new procedures as we abandon old ones. The same can be said for starting a new job, moving to a new address, or engaging in a new relationship. God's relationship with His people changed in some significant ways with the Cross of Christ and the coming of the Holy Spirit. As John puts it, *"For the Law was given through Moses; grace and truth were realized through Jesus Christ."* (Jn.1:17). Note that this is not a system's upgrade but more like a whole new operating system. This is the point of Sarah and Hagar's story as explained by Paul in Galatians.

Christian baptism pictures the installation of this new (spiritual) operating system in our lives. It is all too easy to try to treat the new system like the old and that will not work. God takes our baptism seriously as must we.

Let's look at some of the differences between the Old and New Covenant systems.

Psychological Guilt is Replaced with Godly Sorrow.

It might be helpful to distinguish between legal moral guilt and psychological guilt. The first is an objective legal verdict, while the second is a subjective emotional response to being excluded, rejected, and condemned. Psychological guilt is usually destructive and need not be a part of the Christian experience. The sin of the Christian does not condemn and should not isolate the believer from a sense of God's love. Psychological guilt feelings are not to be confused with the convicting work of the Spirit, which corrects but does not condemn. Condemnation *of the believer* is the work of Satan, not God. Those who walk in the Spirit should not experience toxic, psychological, guilt even though they may be legally guilty.

> ### A point to ponder
> Shame is God's tool before salvation and Satan's tool after.

So what should the believer feel when he or she sins? There certainly should be a sense of sorrow and loss but not exclusion and condemnation. When I sin, I respect the convicting presence of the Spirit of Christ reminding me I am hurting myself. I am also being a hypocrite to my new identity in Christ, and I am grieving the Spirit of the one who paid my way out of such behavior. I do not however feel condemned, excluded from God's family, or shamed into withdrawal from God. My sin does not separate me from God if I am in Christ. Sin is most harmful when it causes me to turn away from God in shame and guilt. Sin should lead me toward Christ, not away from him, even though my natural reaction is to withdraw. If I walk in the Spirit, I walk in the light of grace without fear of drawing near to Christ for mercy, assurance, and help.

Love and grace cast out fear and shame. Peace does not come until fear and shame are removed.

A young man in our congregation experimented with drugs in his early teen years. He knew this was not right and was inconsistent with his family's values. When his parents confronted him, he quickly confessed and said he had meant to talk to them about the issue but did not know how to do it. He shared with them that he felt embarrassed and was sad it had happened. His parents asked him if he was afraid to tell them about it. He responded by assuring them that he was more embarrassed than afraid. The parents wisely wanted him to know the difference between right and wrong but also to know the difference between grace and condemnation. The Spirit of Christ can convict without condemning. The law always condemns those under its influence and promotes fear.

Faithfulness should be Motivated by Grace not Fear.

I can tell a lot about the spirit of a person, a family, a church, a business, and a culture by simply observing the tools it uses to motivate people to appropriate behavior. Guilt, fear, and promise of material reward are effective motivations in the short run; but do they really produce the kind of behavior that glorifies God and edifies people? I am not suggesting that promise of reward and warning against the negative consequences for bad behavior are always inappropriate. There are many biblical examples of warning and promise as a motivation for faithfulness. But Paul is touching a fundamental Christian principle when he says, *"the love of Christ constrains us"* (2 Cor.5:14). We love because He first loved us (1 Jn.4:19). We forgive because we are forgiven (Eph.4:32). We are not conformed to the world because of His mercy (Rom.12:1–2).

As a pastor, teacher, father, husband, and citizen I am challenged to believe that love and grace motivate more powerfully and appropriately than do guilt, fear, and promise of material reward.

> ## *A point to ponder*
>
> As parents we have less control
> of but more influence over
> our teenage children than we think.

At the dinner table one evening a teenage daughter asks this question of her parents: "If I were pregnant and wanted to have an abortion, would you let me?" How is that for a discussion starter? If you were the parent, how would you respond? Let's say that you were quite sure that she is not pregnant. You suspected she had been talking about the subject in school and probably got an earful of horror stories from some of her friends who were afraid their parents would disown them if they faced such circumstances. Hopefully you would realize that you are facing a special moment in your role as a parent. Siblings sitting across the table are waiting eagerly to hear how safe it would be in this family to "color way outside the lines."

Here is what one parent said in just that situation: "If you are old enough to get pregnant, you are old enough to have a big say in how you are going to deal with the responsibilities of pregnancy." The situation would be faced as a family that respected and included each member. If there were disagreements, they would have to be worked out respecting each person's feelings and role. This daughter was assured that she would never be disowned or excluded from the love or the family. This was no time for a morality lecture, nor was it a time for some spiritual talk about God's will. The real question being asked was—how safe is it in this family? And that was the question these parents addressed.

In the same way we sense grace most keenly in the moment of our failure, so do those around us sense our love and grace in our reactions to their failures. This does not mean we are looking for others to fail so they can sense our grace. However we are not to be intimidated or shocked by the failure of others. We are to see failure as an opportunity to show love and grace. This love may involve discipline with a willingness to forgive and restore. When the Apostle Paul disciplined the immoral person in 1 Corinthians 5, his motive was love for the sinner and the community. This is most evident in 2 Corinthians 2 where he encourages the church to respond to a penitent sinner when he says, *"reaffirm your love for him"* (vs.8). We must not be afraid of failure, nor must we be shocked when others fail. Where sin abounds, grace all the more abounds. Grace feeds on our failure and the failure of others. This grace is one virtue that will not be needed in heaven as it is needed in an imperfect world of imperfect people. It is appropriate only where sinners dwell and in that context it is indispensible.

Guidance should come from Principles not Fixed Rules.

How do you make decisions concerning "God's will"? Under grace those decisions are made as a son not a slave. A slave does as he is told without asking why. A son, on the other hand, shares the secrets and goals of the family and thus is given more freedom than a slave in making decisions about what should be done.

As a child I loved to draw and paint. I can remember my parents giving me an oil painting set, with a "paint by the numbers" picture. The canvas board was full of lines and numbers that did not reveal the landscape that would later appear. My job was to match the number on the canvas with the number on the paint jar and stay within the lines. When I finished, the picture emerged—a little crude and mechanical looking, but identifiable and encouraging for a beginner. Several years later when I was drawing a portrait, I had only two guides, the face I was studying and the skill in my hands learned from experience. So it is in life. When we were young and tutored by the law, we painted by the numbers. We lived the Christian life by a set of mechanical (external) rules—give 10 percent, "owe no man anything," "give to all who ask," and so on. As we mature, those rules shape our hearts to embrace a godly perspective on giving that may be more principle driven than rule driven. For example, in Paul's letter to the Corinthian church he does not teach the rule of tithing but advocates the principle of "equality" (2 Cor.8:14) as a guide to determine how much should be given. He is no longer painting by the numbers. In Romans 14 Paul is not insisting that the Sabbath law of the Old Covenant be applied to Saturday worship but gives freedom to the believer to worship on different days (Rom.14:5). In 1 Corinthians 7:39 Paul counsels a wife who has lost her husband to marry *"whom she wishes, only in the Lord."*

Decision Making

Under Old Covenant	Under New Covenant
External guide	Internal guide
Law driven	Spirit led
Follow laws	Follow principles
Looking to others to discern the law for us	Trusting the Holy Spirit to give us inner wisdom
Rigid	Flexible
Fear of making mistakes	Confidence in the love of God

As spiritual sons and daughters we are trusted to use our instincts in making decisions. With the indwelling Holy Spirit we are not given a road map but a compass with freedom to take one of a number of paths to the goal. When Paul counseled the Corinthians in 1 Corinthians 7 about marriage, he did not say; "Pray for a revelation of God's will for the right mate that I have chosen for you." He said, *"My advice is do not marry, but if you do, you have not sinned."* (vs.36) He gave them freedom to make choices within the boundaries of God's purposes. In verse 39 we read, *"A wife is bound as long as her husband lives; but if her husband is dead, she is free to be married to whom she wishes, only in the Lord.*" Note the freedom to choose.

I am not suggesting God never gives direct guidance. But His direct guidance is more the exception than the rule. While the Epistles of the New Testament have a lot to say about God's will, seldom is the advice personally specific. Most of the revelation is "station to station" rather than "person to person." Now to be sure, we who share the Spirit of Christ are expected to know His values, goals, priorities, and ways so we will make wise decisions. James tells us in chapter one of his letter that if we lack *wisdom*, we are to pray for it. He does not call us to pray for a special revelation of God's will but rather for clear insight into our motives and God's values.

Financial Stewardship as an Example.

The Law of Moses is not sufficient to guide us in living under the New Covenant. While it is important we respect the law as holy and good, it is also important for us to realize it cannot produce in us the holiness of heart that God demands for fellowship with Him. A good example of this is seen in the biblical teaching on financial stewardship. Under the Old Covenant of law there were exact prescriptions for giving. Three tithes were mentioned.

1. 10% went to the support of the Levites and the temple ministry (Lev.27:30–33; Num.18:20–21).

2. 10% went for a sacred meal in Jerusalem (Deut.12:17–18).

3. Every third year 30% went for the welfare of the needy (Deut.14:28–29).

The total giving of an Israelite by this reckoning was to be about 25%. Any "freewill" offerings were over and above this 25% required tithe (Deut.12:6,11; 1 Chron.29:6–9,14).

Under the New Covenant the tithe is not prescribed. A much more dynamic and demanding system is called for. Paul explains in 2 Corinthians 8–9:

1. Christians are to give so as to establish a sense of economic equality among believers (2 Cor.8:13).

2. The ability and motivation to give to the Lord is a function of grace (2 Cor.8:1,3,6,7; 9:8–10).

3. In God's eyes the attitude of the giver is more important than the amount given (2 Cor.9:7).

4. The Christian's practice of giving is to be regular, systematic, and proportionate (1 Cor.16:1–2).

These principles are not presented by Paul as a new law but as instructions for life under grace. Be wary of the impulse to "follow rules" that turn these principles into another law system. The Christian who walks in the Spirit is going to know and respect the principle of the law while allowing the Spirit to guide its application. The spirit, not the letter of the law, is the real authority. When Christ healed on the Sabbath, He violated the technical tradition of the Sabbath, but He upheld the spirit of the Sabbath.

Four Criteria Identify a Virtuous Deed.

In order for an act to be truly virtuous—free from the burden of the law—it must respect four criteria: First, it must be consistent with the direct moral teaching of Scripture. For example, husbands who follow Christ are to lay their lives down for their wives as Christ did for the church (Eph.5:25). Second, it must be motivated by love. It is possible to do "the right thing" but, like Jonah, not have our heart in it. Virtue is internally motivated from the heart. Third, it must be timely. For example telling the truth is consistent with the teaching of Scripture, but if the truth is used to slander someone out of spite, it is no virtue. By the same token if the truth is not timely, it can be not only embarrassing but also abusive. Paul reminds us that love *"does not act unbecomingly"* (1 Cor.13:5). It is possible to have loving feelings but act unwisely. A mother who spoils her child may do so with feelings of love in her heart but without wisdom in her actions. A person who seeks to minister to an alcoholic may unwisely give him money because he seems needy (as the Scripture technically suggests). By doing so the giver may be aiding and abetting the alcoholic's addiction. The timing is critical, if it is to be a loving gesture. Fourth, it must be freely chosen and not coerced or manipulated by fear. Note 2 Corinthians 9:7 *"Each one must do just as he has purposed in his heart, not grudgingly or under compulsion, for God loves a cheerful giver."* Doing the right thing from a wrong spirit may help others but not constitute spiritual fruitfulness before God.

Sarah is our true mother.

Sarah is the mother of all who claim the name of Christ. The covenant she represents is a covenant of freedom and peace. It must be received and embraced wholly if we are to experience and express God's radical grace. The benefits of this covenant are great in every way. It frees us from guilt and shame. It takes out of play condemnation and the fear it inspires. It invites us to participate in Kingdom life and ministry not as slaves or children but as adults with freedom to choose and responsibility to follow the principles of Kingdom life. Hagar is a mother who served an important role in our lives, but we now see her in a very different context—through the eyes of faith in Christ. Her story is the subject of the next chapter.

Steps of Application

1. Be honest. Are you living after the spirit of Hagar more than Sarah?
   a. Identify areas of your life that are rule driven.
   b. Are you sensing a freedom in Christ that not only removes fear of punishment but also motivates you to obedience?

2. Identify one area in your life where you are facing an important decision.
   a. What specific "laws," rules, or signs have you used to make important decisions in the past?

    b. How would you expect God to lead you apart from specific signs or rules?

    c. Can you trust God to give you wisdom without specific rules or revelations?

3. List two examples where you had to walk by faith apart from written rules. What has been the result?

4. Where in your life is your flesh most likely to use grace as an excuse for sin? How can you guard yourself against this temptation? What do you plan to do about it?

Questions for Discussion

1. What has God used to bring a sense of His love and grace into your life?

2. How does your church motivate its members? Does it use – love, gratitude, and sincerity or things like fear, guilt, and pride?

3. Give examples of grace from your family life.

4. How do you know that the motivation for behavior is coming from external fear or internal love?

5. Are there parts of this chapter with which you disagree? Why?

Chapter 6
Hagar – She Must Have Her Say, not Her Way

Obstacle #2 to Peace with God: A Legalistic Spirit

To experience peace with God, we must let the law crush our hopes of self-righteousness and lead us to Christ who is our peace.

Rabbi Harold S. Kushner's book *How Good Do We Have To Be?* echoes the sentiment of many religious people saying, "I thought I had to be perfect for people to love me." Where do our perfectionist impulses come from? Should we repress them? Kushner and others would encourage us not to be too hard on ourselves lest we become neurotic.

I believe there is something of the image of God within all humans that aspires to a high level of living. We value this impulse when it motivates us to grow; yet we may hate it when it drives us to obsessive lifestyles. Religion, and especially Christianity, is often blamed for encouraging unrealistic perfectionist tendencies in people. The blame is based on a well-founded principle. An important part of the biblical message is a call to a moral standard, which if taken seriously, would make the average person neurotic. But the moral law of God is neither the problem (Rom.7:7,14) nor the solution (Rom.3:20). The problem is human weakness and sin. The solution is found in Christ's righteousness credited to our account by faith.

While Hagar is pictured in a negative light in Galatians, it is a grave mistake to assume she does not have a vital role in God's plan for His people. However Hagar's role and the law covenant she represents are often misunderstood. If we do not comprehend the meaning of Hagar, we will not appreciate the significance of Sarah. Hagar and the law covenant she represents would eventually be replaced, but it is important she be allowed to tell her story and to carry out her God-ordained mission before she departs. The law like Hagar is not evil, nor is it our enemy. The law is our friend if it is used lawfully, that is according to its God-ordained purpose.

Perfecting Ourselves to Death

A Chinese proverb reminds us *"Even the best needles are not sharp at both ends." Perfectionism: The Road to Heaven or Hell* is the title of Dr. Richard Winter's first lecture on the topic that led to the writing of his helpful book *Perfecting Yourself to Death*. In chapter six he reveals the thought patterns of perfectionists.

First, he notes they have a low tolerance for ambiguity. Life is seen as black or white, all or nothing, and good or bad. They have trouble accepting the gray areas of life. Their sentences have more exclamation points and fewer commas. This discomfort with the "gray" areas of life sets them up for the next thought pattern.

Second, perfectionists tend to be rigid and resistant to change. When change is called for, it presents a problem. If it is gradual, the perfectionist is frustrated because of the all-or-nothing impulse (above). If change is dramatic, it is unsettling because there are too many new and unfamiliar challenges that tend to bring stress. The only hope for peace is to avoid change.

Third, perfectionists suffer from the tyranny of "ought and should." There is a strong need for things to "go right." When they go wrong, someone must take the blame or suffer the shame. Perfectionists have an overly sensitive conscience and a tendency to make everything a matter of right or wrong. There is a right way and a wrong way to put on clothing, do the dishes, correct the children, run the church, etc.

Fourth, they have a fear of making mistakes. This means decision-making is hard because the stakes are so high. Perfectionists avoid risks lest they make a mistake and suffer shame or find themselves on the wrong side of an issue. When there is only black and white, the risks of error can be overwhelming. To minimize mistakes they need rule makers and rule enforcers leading them to the fifth thought pattern.

Fifth, perfectionists are attracted to legalism. In an attempt to keep life under proper management, authoritarian rule makers and enforcers are needed. For the perfectionist guilt and blame are what life is all about in the church, family, and work place. The final characteristic is inevitable.

Sixth, perfectionists tend to deny reality. Winter notes: neurotics have a dream of how they want life to be, psychotics live in the dream they believe is real, and psychiatrists get paid to treat them.

The Law is a Moral Vision for All.

Paul does not teach us that the Law of Moses has been discarded as a moral code or vision. The Law of Moses reflects the nature and glory of a holy, just, and loving God. As a reflection of God's nature, it "abides forever" (Ps.119:152). God's moral character does not change with time or with the New Covenant.

When I was learning to ski, I was taught to concentrate on many details involving the shifting of weight from one foot to another, pressuring the tips of the skis in one direction or another, and thinking ahead as I looked down the slope. After learning to ski, these details became automatic because they were programmed into my subconscious. As a matter of fact once they were learned, I discovered a certain amount of freedom to improvise and do things that were not a part of the initially learned rules. I was free from the rules, but the rules were still true and valuable. My freedom from the rules did not cause me to despise the rules or ignore them. Rather I would frequently go back and review them when my technique wasn't working. In the same way the law as a moral vision remains valuable and holy even when we may not be preoccupied with its details, fear its violation, or hope in its power. When Paul speaks of being free from the law, he is referring to its covenantal power not its value in reflecting the holy nature of God.

The Law is a True but Superficial Ethic.

It might be helpful at this juncture to look at the way God has progressively revealed the moral nature of His kingdom throughout history. God revealed His holy moral character in a general nonspecific sense through nature (the creation, human conscience, and social culture). All humans share some common moral instincts—respect for human life and property, the sanctity of marriage, proscriptions against incest, and a sense of moral accountability.

When Moses articulated the moral law through the Ten Commandments, God codified and clarified that which was latent and nonspecific in creation, conscience, and culture. But this moral code, though clear and specific, was external, superficial, and fell far short of the richness and depth of God's character expressed later in Christ. With the coming of Christ, the fullness of the Godhead was revealed. And with the coming of His Spirit to His people, His divine character would be installed within believers, creating a love impulse that would guide people to godly living from the inside out.

With the coming of Christ, the holy character of God is expressed most perfectly through what is called "the law of Christ." In Hebrews 7:12 we read, *"When the priesthood is changed, of necessity there takes place a change of law also."* This change in law is a change in degree of clarity with a new focus on the inner life of motives and attitudes flowing from the Spirit of Christ installed in the heart of the believer. Later in the same chapter verse 18 we read, *"For, on the one hand, there is a setting aside of a former commandment because of its weakness and uselessness (for the Law made nothing perfect), and on the other hand there is a bringing in of a better hope, through which we draw near to God."* The commandment was good, but the revelation in Christ was better because it rested not on the failed performance of man but on the perfect conformity by Jesus to the law's demands.

Paul refers to this *"law of Christ"* in 1 Corinthians 9:20–21, *"And to the Jews I became as a Jew, that I might win Jews; to those who are under the Law, as under the Law, through not being myself under the Law, that I might win those who are under the Law; to those who are without law, as without law, though not being without the Law of God but under the law of Christ."* We might say the law of Christ upgrades the Law of Moses as a code of conduct. The upgrade displays inner instincts and principles shaped by Christ's Spirit that govern a person's life by love.

Natural Law	*Mosaic Law*	*Law of Christ*
General and nonspecific	Specific but superficial	Inner and radical
Revealed to all through creation, culture, & conscience.	Revealed to Israel through the Old Covenant	Revealed to Christians through the Spirit

So what does this mean for us? First, the Law of Moses as expressed in the Ten Commandments can and should be taught to Christians as a guide to ethics. This can be done while at the same time respecting Paul's teaching about the law's termination as a covenant of works. A wise Christian teacher of the Law of Moses will link it to the life of Christ and expand upon it from his life and the teaching of the apostles. The law is still and always will be holy and good. We should love it, listen to it, learn from it, and live it. But we should not feel as though it can condemn us when we fail to live by it. It can no longer threaten those

95

who have died to it and are clothed with the imputed righteousness of Christ by faith.

Second, when making moral decisions, a mature Christian will not always demand a text from the Bible to give technical sanction to "God's will." The inner instinct of selfless love and worship will guide the believer. The text of the law can and should be a useful checks and balances when seeking to know the way of love. But it is understood that the essence of the Spirit and life of Christ is at work in our minds and hearts guiding us into truth.

A man called me one afternoon with this question: "As a Christian am I permitted to remarry, given I am divorced from my second wife?" While it would be important for me to refer to the technical teaching of Jesus and Paul on this subject, it would be even more important for me to listen to the Spirit of Christ to find wisdom to help this brother. A person living under the law might look for a Biblical text or a technical answer from 1 Corinthians, Matthew, or Deuteronomy. Under grace there is a heavier burden to bear. I am not just interested in the technical aspects of the Biblical standards with respect to divorce and remarriage as important as they are. I am going to probe into other areas of motive, spirit, circumstance, and so on before I decide how to respond to this brother.

Many pastoral matters call for more than the technical reading of the law; they call for a response driven by the indwelling Spirit of Jesus. This is what we might call Godly "wisdom." It does not take us long to realize that in many real life decisions we are faced with conflicting laws or principles. Should I give to everyone who asks out of need? What if they happen to be addicted to drugs and plan to use my gift to continue their habit? Love applied in wisdom may lead me to refuse to give money to such a person. Giving in such a case may very well contribute to their self-destruction. There may be a need to respect the role of "damage control" in facing situations where Biblical standards seem to contradict each other, as is often the case

96

in issues of marriage and divorce. Moral decisions that are motivated by love (seeking the true welfare of another) are often difficult and call for Spirit guided wisdom.

Guidance under

Natural Law	Mosaic Law	Law of Christ
Conscience and social contract	Biblical rule and tradition	Leading of the Spirit through the principles of Scripture

The Law Provides the Context for Understanding Grace.

I once received a bill from my credit card company with an interest charge attached. I had forgotten to pay my last month's bill, resulting in an incurred late fee. Because I have made it a habit to always pay my credit card off at the end of each month, I was irritated with the interest charge of $56. I called the credit card company and asked if the charge could be waived. Without hesitation the young woman on the other end of the line said, "No problem, Mr. Abrahamson. We will take the charge off your bill." These words were music to my ears. I called my wife with the news, "You won't believe this, honey, but they took the charge off our account."

Let's back up and entertain a different scenario—I paid my bill on time and was not guilty. If I were told that the card company was not going to charge me a $56 fine this month, I would have said, "Of course they are not going to charge me. Why would they be charging me in the first place? I have done nothing wrong." My response would not be one of joy but of a deep sense of entitlement. So it is with grace and law in the spiritual world. Grace is not going to be appreciated until we feel the bite of the law and then sense the message of freedom from its intimidating sting. The graciousness of the credit card company was appreciated only in the context of sensing my culpability, vulnerability, and indebtedness. Grace is appreciated in proportion to our awareness of our sin. The law's role as a tutor is to give us that awareness (Rom.7:7–9).

Law is the expression of God's holy character and an imperative upon all who will have fellowship with Him. While we focus attention on the Law of Moses, it should be understood that the whole principle of moral obligation and duty is in view. When Paul speaks of the law, he has in mind the Law of Moses, including the Ten Command-ments. The Reformers rightly defined law as any command, instruction, or exhortation that defines duty—what we should do, how we should live, what we must be. "Love thy neighbor," "Be ye therefore perfect," and "Purify your minds" are examples of law. The "law" is the moral code governing our relationship with God in such a way that by obeying we are blessed and by disobeying we are alienated from God. But in drawing attention to God's holy character, the Law of Moses also exposes our unholy nature. In so doing it creates a hunger for a righteousness that can only come through faith in Christ. The good news is Christ has fulfilled the demands of the law for His people. When we ignore the law, we run the risk of misunderstanding the cross. The law first defines the nature of our bondage and debt. The law then clarifies the role of Christ so we can appreciate His life and death for us.

A point to ponder

It is a serious mistake to ignore the law but a fatal mistake to ignore the cross.

Without the Law of Moses the Cross of Christ can be misunderstood. In Galatians 4:4 Paul tells us Jesus was *"born under the Law so that he might redeem those who were under the Law."* The death of Christ should not be dismissed as simply an example of suffering as a martyr, or an unfortunate miscarriage of social justice. The Cross finds its meaning in the context of the just demands of the law for a sin sacrifice.

The Promise Given to Abraham came Before the Law of Moses.

Three biblical covenants work together to tell the story of God's good news of radical grace. A covenant is a contract, a formal (legal) agreement, as to how a relationship is to be conducted or an estate is to be distributed. When God dealt with His people, He made covenants that provided legal understanding of what was expected from Him and them in the relationship.

The covenant God made with Abraham in Genesis (Gen.12:1–4; 13:14–17; 15:1–7; 17:1–8) is the basis of God's redemptive plan and provides the backbone of the rest of the biblical story of salvation. When the prophets, Jesus, and the Apostles refer to "the promise," it is usually the covenant with Abraham they have in mind. This covenant is unilateral and unconditional. It is "unilateral" because God promises it to Abraham and his seed so as to bless all who are of faith. This blessing is "unconditional" — not conditioned upon human merit or faithfulness.

When my daughter was fifteen, my wife and I would take her to the shopping center parking lot on Sunday afternoons and let her practice driving the family car. These practice sessions were in anticipation of her sixteenth birthday when she would receive her driver's license. We promised her when she turned sixteen, she could receive her license. This promise was unilateral and unconditional. When she turned sixteen, we all knew this would take place even though we had the power to grant or withhold permission to get a license. We also knew no matter how skilled she was as a driver, ready or not; she would be getting the license. This understanding did not mean she would be necessarily driving by herself or whenever and wherever she wanted. When I say this promise was unilateral and unconditional, I am not saying our daughter had no responsibilities before its benefits could be experienced. She would have to go to the state office and pass a driver's test. However the test was not a giant obstacle. The real issue was the permission and sanction of her parents. God's covenant with Abraham was like the promise of a driver's license. Abraham would have to cooperate in order to receive the blessing, but the blessing was not something he could earn or merit through heroic effort. It was a unilateral promise with stipulations.

This covenant with Abraham provides the context for two other covenants that are of great significance in understanding God's redemptive plan. The unilateral and unconditional nature of the promise covenant made with Abraham is important when we contrast it with the conditional nature of the law covenant made through Moses. Paul links the covenant of promise with the covenant of law fulfilled in Christ (Gal.3:8,16).

The Law is a Temporary Covenant.

The covenant at Sinai (Ex.20-31), often called "the law," was given to Israel through Moses with the Ten Commandments. Its purpose was to prepare Israel to identify and respond to the promise given to Abraham. This was a conditional covenant with Israel whereby blessings and curses were related to Israel's obedience or disobedience to over 600 specific commands.

I live in a town with a very successful college basketball program. In the 70s and 80s the coach recruited some of the best high school players in the nation. These players come to Chapel Hill having been the stars of their high school teams and leagues. They were good and they knew it. However, when they came to the ACC and Carolina, they entered a whole new culture. One of the first things the coach did was show them how much they didn't know. He let the freshman scrimmage against the veterans. It wasn't pretty. Big egos got put in their place. The coach knew until players realized how much they fell short, they would not listen to the coach and learn how to play as a team. In a similar way the Law of Moses was given to put us in our place and get us to listen. Its message was not, "If you try harder and learn better technique, you will succeed." The message was, "You cannot meet the requirements of the law; you need deliverance from its demands and penalties."

> ### A point to ponder
>
> We are free from the Law of Moses
> as a covenant but not free from it
> as a guide to Kingdom living.

The Law is Ordained by God for a Tutorial Purpose.

I seldom remember my dreams, but when I do; I often remember what I call the "student's nightmare" dream. In this dream I am enrolled in a calculus class at the university. I have forgotten where the class meets because I have not attended class hoping the class would somehow disappear. But now it is exam week, and I am in high anxiety. If I don't do something, I will get an F; but I don't know what to do. I am not at all prepared for an exam in a class I have not attended. Then I wake up and realize I graduated from college years ago. There are no more exams, and there is no more anxiety. Yes, there was a time when class attendance and exams were important, but no longer. I thank God for mornings after a "student's nightmare" dream. Then I came to realize the moral demands of the law as a covenant were just like that dream, leaving me in fear and hopeless despair. Awakening to grace was like waking after a bad dream and suddenly realizing I was free.

The law covenant was designed to show us three things. First, it revealed our need for a redeemer. Second, it gave meaning to substitutionary sacrifice and the Cross of

Christ. Third, it enabled Israel to identify her Messiah as the one who perfectly embodied the image and nature of God. For these reasons, Paul calls this covenant a *"tutor"* (Gal.3:24). This covenant was designed to teach mankind for a period of time until a new covenant would be formed. This New Covenant is based not on the weakness of human flesh but on the strength of God's Son.

I like to think of the law as training wheels for the Christian life. When training wheels are in place, they keep a bicycle from turning over. After the rider learns to ride the bike, the wheels are removed. The rider is then free to ride without the limitations of the training wheels, but he or she is also free to fall. It is expected however that the rider will not often fall because the training wheels have done their job.

The Tutorial Work of the Law
for Non-Christians

revealing human sinfulness	revealing Christ's holiness	revealing the meaning of the cross
The law produces pain, shame, & longing for Christ.	The law authenticates Christ as a worthy sacrifice.	The law's demand for punishment of sin is fully satisfied.

Jesus' Interpretation of the Law

Jesus was born under the law and lived His life under the law. His teaching is to be understood in that context. The law covenant was in force until the death of Christ at which time it was fulfilled. The cross was the deathblow to both our sins and the law's power to condemn.

It is a mistake to think of Jesus as a "kinder, gentler Moses." He did not come to take the sharp edge off the law and assure us God really didn't mean all those harsh warnings about condemnation and exclusion for those who were disobedient. It was Jesus who said, *"For I tell you that unless your righteousness surpasses that of the Pharisees and the teachers of the Law, you will certainly not enter the kingdom of heaven."* (Matt.5:20). In Matthew 5:17–48 Jesus explains the true moral intent of the law. In the Sermon on the Mount (Matt.5-7), Jesus restores to the law the teeth that the religious leaders of his day had extracted. They had viewed the law as an instrument of comfort and security for all who "kept its demands." What they had failed to realize was: when understood properly, no one could keep the Law perfectly.

Jesus forced people to see the law in such a way, that it convicted and condemned all who stood before it. No one could manage its demands. He interpreted the commandment prohibiting adultery as referring also to lust. He understood the commandment prohibiting murder to refer to anger as well. His exposition forced all to be "poor in spirit," "hungering and thirsting for righteousness." Uncovering our spiritual poverty is precisely what the Law of Moses was designed to do. The law was clarified and explained by Christ in the Sermon on the Mount. Jesus' definition of the law rendered everyone guilty before its demands. It was given to convict, not to comfort. It was to leave us in pain, not in peace.

Some time ago a young man came to me with a painful confession. He was a Christian businessman who had an affair with his boss—a woman who was not a Christian. As he shared his shame, tears ran down his cheeks. His words displayed the depth of his pain. "I am so ashamed. I am so ashamed." He asked, "Can God forgive me; can I forgive myself; will my wife forgive me?" I shared with him I had bad news and good news for him. The bad news was his sin, and as bad as it was, was not the half of it. Adultery was just the tip of the iceberg. He had just been given a glimpse of the dark side of his life, a side that had been hidden from him but not from God. There was so much more that could be revealed. The question was, "Why has it taken this event to break you before God when your old sin nature has been this bad and worse for so long?" That's the bad news. But there is also some good news.

Part of the good news is, God is not shocked by our behavior. God's grace is more than ample to cover our sin. "The fact you are groaning in guilt is a sign you are in a place to glory in grace." Sin is never a blessing, but the shame and guilt of dramatic sin can put us in a place of great insight if we allow ourselves to be broken by the moral law and cleansed by the blood of Christ. Does this mean that this man's wife will forgive him? Perhaps not, but the grace that enables this man to find peace in the wake of his failure can also sustain him through the pain of any rejection.

A point to ponder

God is never shocked by human behavior as we so often are.

The Law is of Works, not Faith.

The law was often related to the "law-of-works" righteousness. In Ezekiel 18:9 we read, "Keep my decrees and laws, for the man who obeys them will live by them. I am the Lord." While it is true individuals have always been saved by faith, it is also true many have been tempted to rely on obedience to the law as an expression of true faith. In so doing they put themselves "under law." While the law in theory promised life through perfect obedience, it was never intended to work as a vehicle for attaining life. Nonetheless, the law contains an implicit promise of eternal life for those who "do it." In Romans 10:4–5 we read, "For Christ is the end of the law for righteousness to everyone who believes. For Moses writes that the man who practices the righteousness which is based on law shall live by that righteousness." Again in Romans 7:10, "And this commandment, which was to result in life, proved to result in death for me." Other texts link the keeping of the law with eternal life (Matt.19:17; Rom.2:13; Lev.18:5; Phil.3:9; Deut.4:1,8; 27:26; 28:58–59). In Galatians 2:16 Paul makes it clear this promise of salvation by works is hypothetical, for no one can keep the law so as to gain eternal life. "By the works of the Law shall no flesh be justified."

While the Law of Moses is a legitimate expression of God's nature, it is not a legitimate expression of His covenant with those who are in Christ. Paul speaks of Christ's termination of the law as a covenant in the following passages:

> **Colossians 2:14**, *"Having canceled out the certificate of debt consisting of decrees against us and which was hostile to us; and he has taken it out of the way, having nailed it to the cross."*

> **2 Corinthians 3:11**, *"For if that which fades away (vs.7 "the ministry of death, in letters engraved on stones") was with glory, much more that which remains is in glory."*

> **Ephesians 2:15**, *"by abolishing in his flesh the enmity, which is the Law of commandments contained in ordinances,"*

> **Galatians 3:19**, *"Why the Law then? It was added because of transgressions, having been ordained through angels by the agency of a mediator, until the seed should come . . ."*

When Abraham sought Hagar in a works-based attempt to fulfill God's plan for blessing, the choice represented his fleshly pursuit. This is precisely what the law encourages in those who put themselves under its covenant promises and demands. Hagar's life, while pertinent to God's unfolding story of redemption, was not God's ultimate or best plan. The law could not and did not fulfill what God had in mind. Applying this to our lives today (by pursuing works through our own efforts) will not result in the holiness necessary for eternal life. And as we must see, neither will the working of God's Spirit to fulfill the law's demands be the basis of our peace. Christ did not die (primarily) to empower us to fulfill the demands of the Old Covenant ourselves. He died to free us from having to fulfill it to be reconciled to God through Christ.

Help in Application

1. Conduct a spiritual audit of your life. Provide some specific examples of how your life reflects a proper or improper relationship to the law.

2. Pray for insight as you face the challenge of freedom and responsibility before the law.

3. Go back and revisit the demands of the law with the prospect of developing a fresh appreciation for Christ and what he came to do.

Questions for Discussion

1. How would you summarize the role of Hagar?

2. In what ways can the Law of Moses be a helpful or unhelpful guide for our lives?

3. How would you understand Jesus' teaching on forgiveness in Matthew 6:14–15?

4. Are there parts of this chapter with which you disagree? Why?

Chapter 7
Get that Woman (Hagar) Out of Your House

The law continues to condemn all who are under it.

Several years ago a letter came across my desk, and I kept a copy because it seemed to strike a note with the heart of so many Christians I have met.

"I invented an impossible God, and I had a nervous breakdown. I believed in grace, I even taught it. But my real feelings about the God I lived with day by day did not correspond with my teaching. My God was non-gracious and could not be pleased. God's demands of me were so high, and His opinion of me was so low, there was no way for me to live except under His frown ... All day long He nagged me. "Why don't you pray more? Do this. Don't do that. Yield, confess, work harder." God was always using His love against me. He'd show me His nail-pierced hands, and then He would look at me glaringly and say, "Well, why aren't you a better Christian? Get busy and live the way you ought to." Most of all, I had a God who down underneath considered me to be less than dirt. Oh, He made a great ado about loving me, but I believed that the day-to-day love and acceptance I longed for could only be mine if I let Him crush nearly everything that was really me. When it came down to it, there was scarcely a word, or a feeling, or a thought, or a decision of mine that God really liked."

The fact of the matter for most of us is we know enough of the law of God through our conscience and His Word to be tried, convicted, and condemned. When we fight the law, it always wins. If I read Paul's letter to the Galatians correctly, it is supposed to be that way. However we still tend to look to the law and its challenge to live a perfect life as a path to peace and acceptance.

107

Signs that Hagar is in our house

Four signs suggest that Hagar may be somewhere lurking in our house. The first signs are anger and fear. The law will always leave us anxious and often angry. Second, scorekeeping and judgmental attitudes will be common. Under the law we are constantly keeping a record of our performance and the performance of others. The excuses for sinful behavior will abound. Life under the law and its preoccupation with our performance tempts us to "cook the books" of our own story in order to ease the dissonance between what we should do and what we actually do. Four, shame and embarrassment will be present. When we are under the law, we will be embarrassed by what we say or do when it is inappropriate or sinful because it is unsafe to be honest. We spend our time living to protect an image that we feel will be acceptable to a world under the law. When we fall short, we should feel sorrow, pain, remorse, and disappointment but not shame or its more domesticated little brother—embarrassment.

By way of contrast a life free from the law will be confident and gracious. It will be forbearing and patient. It will be quick to acknowledge failure as such. It also will be at peace with the truth of who and where we are in the process of spiritual formation. It will even live with our failures and imperfections as we rest in Christ.

Life in Hagar's House is Terrifying.

The subject of Romans 7 is the power of the law over all who live under it. Living under the law is defined as living with our eyes on our performance as the basis of our spiritual standing before God. Paul saw himself as a "wretched man" in the law's condemning clutches. He found no comfort in moral discipline, spiritual anointing, or penitent renewal. It took death to set him free, the death of Christ that Paul shared in his baptism. Death was the only escape to joy and peace. Life in the Spirit was by definition life free from the law and its scorekeeping of the flesh. It was not only death that freed Paul, but also the realization that the law had been fully satisfied and now terminated as a covenant of works. Christ does not give us joy and peace by empowering us to live "under the law." He frees us from the Law through baptism into His death.

In Romans 7 and 8 Paul explains what happens when the believer puts himself under the law by looking to it for security. He summarizes his argument in 8:6, *"For the mind set on the flesh is death, but the mind set on the Spirit is life and peace."* When we examine our lives through the law, we discover that the law will only condemn our flesh to death. *"For sin, taking opportunity through the commandment, deceived me, and through it killed me"* (Rom.7:11). In such a condition we are *"wretched"* (Rom.7:24). It is only as we set our minds on our new position in Christ that we gain life and peace.

Those who are constantly trying to measure their conduct by the law will never have peace. To use the law lawfully, Christians must not use it as a measure of their relationship with God but rather as a helpful (though superficial) guide for worshiping God with their lives. We may be liberated from the Law of Moses but not from the character of Christ. We may be free from the law, but we are bound by love. If I put myself under the law's authority, it will have the same condemning effect whether I am a non-believer or believer. When I allow my sense of God's love to be conditioned on how faithful I am to living a selfless life of perfect motives and actions, I am under the Law and will not have peace.

Several years ago I would have asked, "But how is this attitude of freedom from the law to help me in my battle with the flesh? How can I have victory over the flesh with its lusts, habits, and power?" For years my prayer was for more discipline until I realized by the very question I was asking, I was putting myself under the law. I wanted by any means possible to perform the works of the law so I wouldn't need to ask forgiveness anymore. I was looking to grace (not law) as the tutor. I wanted to "outgrow" grace. I wanted to be free from grace—not needing it any more. I wanted to be bound to the law. I wanted what every good Pharisee wanted, a record I could be proud of and a life needing little or no forbearance or forgiveness from God or others.

> ### A point to ponder
> The law is our tutor to faith in Christ not vice versa.

In Romans 9:30–10:13 Paul makes it clear that the righteousness demanded by the law could not be achieved through human effort by the flesh or the Spirit. It could only be achieved through faith in Christ who fulfilled the law perfectly. The Gentiles who believed were therefore better off before God than the Jews who were disciplined but not broken under the law. Paul summarizes with these words in Romans 10:3–5, *"For not knowing about God's righteousness, and seeking to establish their own, they did not subject themselves to the righteousness of God. For Christ is the end of the law for righteousness to everyone who believes. For Moses writes that the man who practices the righteousness which is based on law shall live by that righteousness."*

Grace means we find our confidence not in our ability to manage the demands of the law but in our faith in Christ. Our victory over sin is not through a new power to keep the law but rather through faith, faith that Jesus' righteousness is ours. That is to say, the righteousness of his perfect life is imputed to us. We must accept our defeat in the flesh and overcome guilt not with moral renewal but with death and faith. Liberation is by faith not works. Thus we have victory even though we still may sin in the flesh. As we experience this sense of freedom from condemnation, we also experience a transformation of our desire and ability to actually think and behave as God would desire.

In Galatians 2:16–4:7 Paul takes this one step further by exhorting his readers to see themselves as free from the Old Covenant. He is not suggesting the moral demands of the law no longer represent the nature and will of God. He is saying the power to condemn or reward, which was a part of the Old Covenant, no longer applies. The believer is no longer graded on the basis of his performance before the moral law. When we put others or ourselves under the law so as to submit to its promise of reward and punishment for obedience or failure, we will not find the peace our hearts seek.

The law can continue to be a helpful guide to our faith, which is active through love (Gal.5:6) or it can be an instrument of condemnation for those who live under it. Grace means we are free from the law as a covenant of works (rewards and punishments) but bound by love, which in the end fulfills the moral standards of the law. Grace means we are free from the curse and control of sin as well as condemnation for sins. Liberation is from the covenant curse of the law but not from its moral vision.

The following table summarizes the dire results of living by (under) the law as a Christian.

The Terrorizing Work of the Law in the Christian Life

Challenging the strong to live by the flesh	Condemning the sensitive to shame	Hardening the religious to pride
"the mind set on the flesh is death"	"Wretched man that I am"	"Eat not, touch not"

So we summarize our relationship with the moral law of God as expressed in the Ten Commandments in this way. The Law of Moses is given to stir up our "soul sorrow" to the point of longing for Christ. In this sense the pain of guilt and shame is "good news" when it draws our attention to our Savior through our sin. If we do not have a clear picture of God's moral order, we will not appreciate the righteousness of Christ (Heb.7:26–29). If we do not understand the substitutionary sacrifice, we will not appreciate the ransom of Christ (Jn.1:29). If we have no sorrow over our sin, we will have no appreciation of the resurrection of Christ (Rom.4:25). If we have no sense of bondage, we will have no appreciation of the Sabbath "rest" that is in Christ by faith (Gal.5:1-6). The law covenant was given *"because of transgressions"* to expose the "pain of sin." This includes the pain in our hearts (shame and guilt, Rom.3:19–20), the pain in the blood sacrifices of Israel (Heb.9:22), and the pain in the life of Jesus at the cross (Rom.3:24). As "a tutor" the law covenant enables us to know the law of redemption in Christ. It should develop within us a hunger for righteousness, an understanding of substitutionary sacrifice, and a longing for freedom—a freedom we find through faith in Christ.

But Isn't the Spirit given to Fulfill the Law through Me?

Has God given us His Spirit so that we can fulfill the demands of the law? Many Christians believe that He has. It is not strange to find disciples of Christ who say something like this: "Christ paid for the sins committed before I came to faith, but upon receiving the power of Christ's Spirit, I am able and responsible to fulfill the demands of the law." After all, isn't the Spirit's job centered in bringing resurrection power to my experience?

In John's Gospel (ch.15-17) just before Jesus left his disciples to be crucified, he taught them about the Spirit who would come later. In this teaching Jesus outlines the ministry of the Holy Spirit and gave us perhaps the single most important revelation explaining the role of the Spirit.

The Spirit is a *paraclete* or helper (Jn.16:7) who comes alongside to guide us in three areas. The first ministry of the Spirit is to call us to faith as he convicts us of our need for Christ (Jn.16:8). The Spirit uses the law to awaken a hunger and thirst for personal holiness—a righteousness that we do not have and cannot produce. The second ministry of the Spirit is to glorify Christ (Jn.15:26; 16:14) by testifying of his atoning work where he takes our sin and offers us his righteousness by faith. The Spirit comforts us with the assurance of forgiveness and the imputation of righteousness through faith in Christ. The third ministry of the Spirit is to teach the whole truth of the Gospel story which was not explained by Jesus (Jn.16:12) because the story needed to follow the events of the crucifixion and resurrection before it would make sense.

The theme of Jeremiah's prophecy concerning the New Covenant (31:31-34) foretells the Spirit's ministry by making similar points—God's law will be written on our hearts, we will be forgiven of our sins, and we will know the Lord. The writer of Hebrews quotes Jeremiah 31:31-34 (Heb.10:16-17) as an illustration of his point: "*For by one offering He has perfected for all time those who are sanctified.*" (Heb.10:14). The focus is not on our performance but on what Christ has finished in presenting himself for sacrifice as a sin offering. The Spirit's first and primary ministry is in service of the Gospel not the law. He comforts us with Christ's righteousness *for us* before he calls us to walk in Christ's power *through us*.

Will Personal Perfection Solve my Problems?

One of the great lies of the perfectionist quest is, "*If I can only do everything right, people will love me and life will work for me.*" The greatest debunker of this lie is the story of Jesus. Here is a man who knew no sin, understood others completely, lived out His calling perfectly, and yet was misunderstood, persecuted, despised, and eventually crucified. Now **if** Jesus was treated with such injustice, what makes me think I can solve my problems by being perfect?

What is a "Pharisee Spirit?"

When I first came to a serious commitment of my life to Christ, I was a student at Iowa State University. My commitment was really a series of commitments, a process of being convinced in my mind, won over in my heart, and exercised in my walk. After four years of college I was dead serious about my faith and on my way to seminary. As a young believer I heard a lot of testimonies, read lots of books, and received loads of advice from friends, pastors, and mentors. In the whole process there was one driving impulse motivating most of my inquiry into the faith. It is expressed in my most commonly uttered prayer, "Lord, give me the desire and discipline to live a life of victory."

For years I tried to do just that. I knew all about the love and grace of God, but I had this notion that after two years of growth I should be at the place where I no longer needed so much grace. I was tired of asking for forgiveness and weary of trying every new four-step or twelve-step program that promised freedom from sin. As I look back on my early life, I realize I really was trying to be a Pharisee. I wanted to please God. I wanted to live by faith and under grace so that I could obey the law's demands from the inside out. My testimony was one of frustration and confusion as I found no relief. I literally wore out the pages in my Bible at Romans 6–8. They were so worn from my wrestling with their contents that they became hard to read. I read every book I could get my hands on that had anything to do with "victory over sin."

It wasn't that I was a big-time sinner in the world's eyes. As a matter of fact most people who knew me would say I had it all together. I was in a fraternity and didn't drink, smoke, or experiment with drugs. I dated nice girls and went to church. I didn't even feel proud. In fact pride was the furthest thing from my Christian experience. But as I read the demands of the law expressed by Christ, I was still constantly convicted, no, *condemned* for falling short.

Some might say, "You shouldn't be so hard on yourself. Aren't most 'first born' like yourself struggling with similar issues? After all no one is perfect—right?" I would not have been comforted by such attempts at encouragement. I was taking the Scripture seriously. I read in 1 Corinthians 6:10 that among those who would not inherit the kingdom of God were not only the fornicators, idolaters, adulterers, homosexuals, and so on, but also the "covetous." Poring over the Scriptures I became more and more confused. As I grew in my commitment to Christ, I found this nagging sense of moral imperfection did not depart with increased knowledge of the Bible or faith in God. There was never enough discipline to cover all the demands. I sensed I was trapped in a body of sin that could never be managed in this life except through a superficial understanding of God's expectations or massive denial of my experience. I would always be in need of grace. With Paul in Romans 7 I was a "wretched man." Little did I know I was doing just fine in my preparation to experience the grace of God expressed in Romans.

As I prayed for more discipline, I was praying with the spirit of a Pharisee—focusing on *the law and my obedience* to it. The person who has focused his life on moral discipline is closely related to the person who lives a life of lawless hedonism in that both start and end with the self. But all this has changed. Now I pray for more faith, not with the expectation faith will bring more discipline, but rather that faith will bring a clearer confidence in Jesus as my victory and peace. I suspect I do have more discipline in some areas than I did twenty years ago, but then again that is not the issue. I am a long way from becoming perfect, but I have found my life hidden in one who is perfect. God, who justifies the ungodly by faith, calls them "saints" even when they are acting like "natural men" of the world. This God sets His people "free from the curse of the law." There is a deeper pride than that which is boasting of one's merits. It is a pride that comes from insisting on finding one's way apart from the righteousness of faith.

I realize that much of what I am saying is controversial, risky, and scary. I am maintaining that radical grace has not been properly understood until people ask, "If I am as free as you suggest, will I not go wild and sin without restraint?" The message of radical grace that Paul taught inspired such a fear and thus the question (Rom.6:1).

A point to ponder

When God reveals His grace to us, He takes a risk that we will just taste it and walk away to abuse the freedom it offers.

Sometimes we use the term "cheap grace" to refer to God's promise of blessing without our promise to obey. The grace of God is not cheap, but the first and greatest cost is not to us. The price of grace is the cross. This is not to suggest that grace should not motivate us to gratitude, graciousness, and goodness in living. It should inspire holiness, but at this point I want us to feel the full weight of just how good the news of God's grace really is. Too often grace is little different than camouflaged law, while faith is equated with faithfulness.

The Law Must Be Used Lawfully.

Paul does not tell people to ignore the law but rather to use it properly. *"But we know that the Law is good, if one uses it lawfully, realizing the fact that law is not made for a righteous man, but for those who are lawless and rebellious for the ungodly and sinners"* (1 Tim.1:8–9). Jesus added, *"every scribe who has become a disciple of the kingdom of heaven is like a head of a household, who brings out of this treasure things new and old."* (Matt.12:52)

While God's ultimate plan has always been motivated by grace, and while signs of grace are in the Old Covenant; it is fair to say the Old Covenant of law, like Hagar, is to be cast out with respect to the Christian era with its New Covenant promises and stipulations. Let me reiterate again however that by casting out the Old Covenant, we are not nullifying its moral precepts that reflect the eternal character of a holy God. The Ten Commandments have a place in the Christian's life as a revelation of God's holy nature. The Ten Commandments are superficial, in that Christ deepens and broadens our understanding of the nature of God reflected in the commandments. So we say the Mosaic Law is both "spiritual" (Rom.7:14) and an instrument of death (Rom.2:28–29; 7:6; 2 Cor.3:5–7). It is both "upheld" by the gospel of faith (Rom.3:31) and no longer the "supervisor" of those who have faith (Gal.3:25).

Here you and I face an important question. Before the Law are we outlaws, convicts, or liberated by Christ? If we are outlaws (feeling no responsibility before a holy God), we need to feel the weight of the law and be convicted of a root sin problem we cannot manage or repress. As convicts (feeling guilt, shame, and alienation from God), we need to see the face of our Redeemer and by faith accept our freedom. As liberated (sensing our full acceptance by faith), we need to eagerly live our lives for the one who set us free with the Law guiding us.

Three Positions Before the Law

Outlaws	Convicts	Liberated
feel no responsibility to the law	feel condemned by the law	feel free from the law
need to be convicted	need to be free	called to obey

But some of us are feeling more like parolees. We see ourselves as free but on probation. As soon as we mess up, we sense we will lose our liberty. The good news of the gospel is that with the termination of the law covenant, something has changed to make it impossible for us to ever go back to prison. For we who are in Christ by faith have died with Christ. Our violation of the law was not concealed but fully exposed. The charges against us were not dropped but brought before the judgment of God. The verdict was not acquittal but conviction. The sentence was not commuted, but rather the sentence was carried out. The execution was performed not on us but on Christ for us. With Christ's death the demands of the law for justice and death were fulfilled. Furthermore the law itself as a covenant was terminated. Its court was closed. Probation is not one of the options for us who are in Christ. We are not convicted felons who have limited rights because of our past status as convicts. We are new creatures in Christ. Our baptism is a picture of death and a new birth.

> ### *A point to ponder*
>
> Death is the only sure escape
> from the Law's condemnation.

We are dead to the law since we are no longer condemned by it or find assurance through it. Death is the only way to escape the law, and those who cling to Christ by faith are baptized into His death. Radical grace takes us out from under the law. It calls us to live without fear of condemnation and to stand in awe of God's power toward us in Christ by following Him.

As Christians we are not to put ourselves over the law by becoming a law unto ourselves, nor are we to put ourselves under the law by staying in bondage to its condemnation, nor are we to be outside the law by not letting it guide us in our desire to be authentic followers of Christ. We are to be free from the law in the sense that its power to condemn is over, its appeal to our flesh is broken, and its standard for fellowship with God is satisfied in Christ apart from our performance.

Three Mistakes we can make In our Relationship with the Law

Live Above the Law	*Live Under the Law*	*Live Outside the Law*
I have no respect for God or myself as His image-bearer.	I seek to gain and keep God's favor through obedience to the Law.	I use my freedom to feed the lusts of the flesh.
A seared conscience is the result.	Guilt or pride is the result.	Divine discipline is the result.

A high price is paid when we fail to kick Hagar out of our house. God's peace will not exist in her presence. But the price is even higher if we do not respect her role—which is to point us to Sarah, the promise of grace. The Law is designed to teach us about ourselves, about our Savior, and about our salvation. If properly understood the Law will reveal our desperate need for a Savior, it will show us how to identify our Savior, and it will prepare us to understand the meaning of the cross as a substitutionary sacrifice. In these respects the law is a holy blessing to be deeply appreciated and studied.

A point to ponder

Christians must live free from the law, not above the law, under the law, or outside the Law.

Help in Application

1. Allow the full demand of the holy nature of God to convict your soul.
   a. Make a list of those "virtues" in your life where you feel most "righteous", and then ask God to show you the true motives behind those areas of relative strength.
   b. Identify and acknowledge as sin all areas of your life that are tainted by selfishness, pride, and fear.
   c. Go through the Sermon on the Mount (Matt.5– 7) and allow Jesus' teaching to uncover your motives and behaviors.

2. Identify areas of pride that come from a superficial interpretation of God's moral law or that come form a spirit of independence from God's grace.

3. Review the material in this chapter and then tell the spirit of Hagar to leave your life with her children— guilt, shame, fear, pride, and intimidation.

4. Thank God for the radical grace He has provided for you in Christ.

Questions for Discussion

1. How can the Ten Commandments be used or misused in the Christian church?

2. Are believers to fear the condemnation of the law in their relationship with God? Why or why not?

3. How is a person to repent from living under the law?

4. How would you summarize the message of this chapter?

5. Are there parts of this chapter with which you disagree? Why?

Section III

Grace and Faith

The Story of Two Fathers: Abraham and Satan

Radical Grace is experienced through living faith.

The Christian life is to be lived from the inside out, from the personal to the social, from the heart through the head and hands, and from the family to the church and the world.

It is important to move beyond an explanation of grace and peace to sharing a personal experience of grace and peace. The doctrines of grace and peace are of little value if not applied to life. Jesus and the apostles not only taught the radical nature of God's love and grace, they also saw the need to pray that we would sense the love of God and have our eyes opened to our identity in Christ. This brings us to the third section in our study of radical grace where we will explore the nature and role of faith as it relates to grace and peace.

One Spirit, One Goal, and Many Paths

God's grace and peace are experienced in several different ways. Some people receive God's grace upon hearing it explained. They see, believe, and start a new walk of faith free from guilt, fear, and pride. The means may be a sermon, a book, a conversation with a friend, or personal study of Scripture that makes the difference. Others will hear grace explained and still feel blocked from the freedom that it promises. My observation reminds me that God's Spirit uses different means to reach different people. Some of the more common channels I have observed will perhaps ring true with your experience.

121

Suffering

One of the most common means of grace we will encounter is also one of the least popular. It is "suffering." There are those who might suggest that without suffering, growth in grace will not take place. I hope that is not true. But my experience suggests there may be greater blessings in pain than we want to believe.

Anyone who has experienced personal failure, lost a child or a mate, or suffered from physical injury or disease knows how powerful such experiences can be in challenging the way we view life. Pain seems to do one of two things. It brings a breakthrough in our growth, or it brings a breakdown in our progress. Pain can bring us peace or make us bitter, but it will affect us in some way.

Dramatic Encounter

Another means of grace for many people is a dramatic encounter with God's Spirit. This often comes in the context of a "charismatic experience."

One friend who had suffered with depression and fear for many years reported a sense of God's love during a charismatic meeting that changed his life. He had never known God's love as he did through this special encounter. My observation has been that such charismatic experiences are usually long lasting in their effect. People really get the point of God's love.

Unfortunately with such dramatic encounters there is a tendency to assume God always and only works in this way. History testifies otherwise. We would all welcome an instant dramatic touch by God, but we will not all have such an experience. Nor should we believe we have the responsibility to create such an encounter. The Spirit blows where He wills and in the way He wishes. I sense that those who question the authenticity of dramatic charismatic encounters are often reacting to the way it is presented as the only way to power and peace.

Therapy

Therapy and counseling can be another means to experience God's grace. I know several believers who have found great freedom through the help of a well-trained therapist. And I might add it is not only "Christian" counseling that can open us to the grace of God.

A dear sister spent four years with a secular counselor who did not understand the faith of her client but was able to help her be open to the love of God. The result was as dramatic and life changing as any "charismatic encounter" I have seen. Another friend is a Christian therapist today because of the life changing effects of his own experience in therapy. He told me, "I did not know peace, spiritual freedom, and God's love until I went through therapy. I did not find this freedom in seminary, Bible memory, or ministry to others." God has a way of working through channels we may not expect.

Sacraments

Another common channel of God's grace is the rich liturgical (sacramental) tradition of the Anglican and Orthodox faiths. Some evangelicals do not believe God can use holy water and priestly blessings to dispense spiritual freedom, but God sometimes goes ahead and uses the sacraments without our permission or recognition.

I have a number of evangelical Roman Catholic friends who are committed to the Roman church and love Jesus. The reason some of them have not become Protestants is not because they do not share Luther's theology of justification by faith, but rather because they have been deeply touched by God through the sacraments of the church. They have encountered the living, loving Christ in the liturgical tradition of their church. They have experienced a depth in prayer through the aesthetic sensitivity of the liturgy.

Family and Church

For many of us the best channel of grace is a loving, healthy family and church. We catch grace by seeing, feeling, and living with it. I once asked a young missionary about the family where she grew up. Her father was a pastor, and three of her brothers and sisters were in vocational Christian work. "Did any of you ever go through a period of rebellion?" I asked. She answered, "Yes, but we could never deny the reality of God's love in our parent's lives. It kept us coming back." One person put it this way: "I have seldom doubted that God loved me and I have sensed that love at a level that controlled my life. This comes in part from my home where I sensed God's love and saw my parents' lives of faith in response to it."

Teaching

Teaching is perhaps the most common means of grace mentioned in Scripture. While I can identify with many of the paths mentioned above, I have come to experience God's grace primarily through exposure to the teaching of the apostle Paul. My experience was not unlike that of Luther who saw the light as he read Paul's writings. I teach the Bible perhaps for that reason. It was the instrument God's Spirit used to bring the grace and peace of God to my soul. The more I wrestled with my own inability to live under the law, the more I saw the light of what Paul was saying about the righteousness of faith. The repentance that would lead to life for me was the turning from one central sin—that sin being self-sufficiency. My exposure to God's grace was through the Biblical story of the Gospel as Spirit led teachers faithfully unpacked it.

Faith

No matter how God's Spirit touches a person's life with the Gospel of grace, there is one common response that is present in everyone who receives the message—faith. The kind of faith that turns the grace of God into personal peace is not a faith in self, or faith in fiat, or faith in faith, nor is it faith in religion. The faith that counts is a response to Christ that can only be described as a deeply personal, penitent, transfer of trust from self or some other source of hope to Christ. Those who know God as their Father will notarize that fact by responding to the person, words, and works of Christ with heartfelt trust. Jesus met many people who had a zeal for religion and God but did not receive him or his teaching. Their faith was not the kind of faith that linked them to God's redeeming grace.

The eighth chapter of John will be the point of reference for our last two chapters as we look at the role of faith in experiencing grace. Verse 31 begins as follows:

John 8:31–47

"31 Jesus therefore was saying to those Jews who had believed Him, "If you abide in My word, {then} you are truly disciples of Mine; 32 and you shall know the truth, and the truth shall make you free." 33 They answered Him, "We are Abraham's offspring, and have never yet been enslaved to anyone; how is it that You say, 'You shall become free'?" 34 Jesus answered them, "Truly, truly, I say to you, everyone who commits sin is the slave of sin. 35 And the slave does not remain in the house forever; the son does remain forever. 36 If therefore the Son shall make you free, you shall be free indeed. 37 I know that you are Abraham's offspring; yet you seek to kill Me, because My word has no place in you. 38 I speak the things which I have seen with {My} Father; therefore you also do the things which you heard from {your} father." 39 They answered and said to Him, "Abraham is our father." Jesus said to them, "If you are Abraham's children, do the deeds of Abraham. 40 But as it is, you are seeking to kill Me, a man who has told you the truth, which I heard from God; this Abraham did not do. 41 You are doing the deeds of your father." They said to Him, "We were not born of fornication; we have one Father, {even} God." 42 Jesus said to them, "If God were

---

your Father, you would love Me; for I proceeded forth and have come from God, for I have not even come on My own initiative, but He sent Me. 43 Why do you not understand what I am saying? {It is} because you cannot hear My word. 44 You are of {your} father the devil, and you want to do the desires of your father. He was a murderer from the beginning, and does not stand in the truth, because there is no truth in him. Whenever he speaks a lie, he speaks from his own {nature;} for he is a liar, and the father of lies. 45 But because I speak the truth, you do not believe Me. 46 Which one of you convicts Me of sin? If I speak truth, why do you not believe Me? 47 He who is of God hears the words of God; for this reason you do not hear {them,} because you are not of God.'"

We can make a number of observations from this passage. First, not all who "believe" are truly "of God." Jesus begins this passage by addressing *"those Jews who had believed him."* It is possible to have a faith that is common to Satan (Jas.2:19). He ends the passage by telling them *"you are not of God."* The material between these verses sifts true faith from false faith. Second, the critical difference between true and false faith was not the depth of sincerity, the disciplined acts of charity, or the religious zeal; but it was the response to the person, words, and work of Jesus. Third, the Jews claimed to be of their father Abraham; but Jesus points out that they were not acting like it. Abraham is the father of faith (Rom.4:1–25), and these Jews were not receiving or believing Jesus. True children of Abraham would believe as Abraham believed. In the preceding passage (vs.21-30) Jesus speaks of his deity, his impending death and resurrection, and the necessity of faith for salvation. Although verse 30 says that many came to believe in him, it was evident from verses 31-47 that they were not buying into his message. Believing in Jesus means buying into and trusting his message. True children of

Abraham are justified by a personal, persevering faith in the sacrificial death and resurrection of the God/Man Christ.

Satan as Father	*Abraham as Father*
Do not believe the Gospel	Believe the Gospel
Murder the truth	Embrace the truth
Self-deception	True to self
Reject Christ	Receive Christ
Judaizers	Christians

Before we look more closely at the relationship between grace and faith, let's take the following inventory. Choose between the two statements "a" or "b." Which best describes your understanding?

1.

(a) A Christian is any person who follows the ethical teachings of Christ.

(b) A Christian is identified by his personal faith in Christ more than by his attachment to religion or the church.

2.

(a) The faith of my parents and my church does not automatically transfer to me. I must deal with the gospel personally.

(b) I am a Christian because I was born into a Christian home and baptized into the church as an infant.

3.

(a) All religions can be boiled down to one simple ethic—love one another.

(b) Christianity is unique in that it does not start with and is not centered on ethical teaching or behavior.

4.

(a) It is arrogant and narrow-minded to claim that Jesus is the only way to God.

(b) Christianity has always recognized that it is exclusive and unique among the religions of the world.

5.

(a) God will not condemn people who try hard to live a life of love toward others.

(b) God does not grade on a curve and demands that all be completely holy if they are to see Him.

6.

(a) My relationship with God rests with the goodness of Christ and my faith in him, not MY good conduct.

(b) If I seek to live a good life, God will accept me.

7.

(a) Because I have had a powerful charismatic experience with Jesus, I must be "in Christ."

(b) I realize that my religious experiences, no matter how powerful, are no substitute for a faith commitment.

8.

(a) True faith always reveals itself through faithfulness to the law.

(b) True faith usually leads to faithfulness but not always in every area of life.

9.

(a) If I feel and believe that God loves and accepts me, that means He does.

(b) My security rests in the gospel not in my feelings.

NOTE:

The (a) statements represent a lie about true faith while the (b) statements represent a more accurate understanding in all but #2,6 where it is just the reverse.

Chapter 8
Abraham – The Father of Faith

Step #3 to Peace with God:
A Spirit of Faith

*To experience peace with God, we
must walk by faith, not by sight.*

Among the unique opportunities afforded a pastor of a
large congregation in a university community is the chance
to address some very interesting groups. I have been invited
by professors in various departments at UNC to give
lectures in their classes. This often led to invitations to
speak in other settings where I almost always felt I was
asked to participate with others who were way above my
intellectual pay grade. One such meeting found me
addressing a group of Fulbright Scholars who met twice a
year in the home of one of its members where they would
ask an outside speaker to address them on some subject of
interest. I had worked with one of these individuals at the
Institute of Humanities in the Research Triangle Park, and
he invited me to address the subject of a Christian response
to the secular university. I was flattered and welcomed the
opportunity. I spoke for about forty-five minutes and then
received questions.

I started by stating my thesis – "Higher education in
American has adopted a radical secularism which is
undermining its commitment to 1) humanism and 2) to the
basic idea of a university." I then explained: " In removing
God and any notion of transcendent (over arching)
authority as a grand narrative, it has lost its vision of the
human soul and with it any hope of finding a unifying story
to link various branches of learning to a cohesive whole.
The university ceases to be authentically humanistic when
it reduces human spirituality (that which makes humans
distinct from animals) to a branch of anthropology or
sociology. Modern universities no longer seek a unifying

story but rather are a loosely associated community of independent departments operating in intellectual isolation from one other. All seem to share the notion that anything outside the umbrella of "science" has no authority, yet each department has its own understanding of how to apply the scientific method. The departments seem unaware of what is being done in other areas of learning. The idea of a Renaissance Scholar integrating knowledge from several key disciplines is viewed as idealistic at best and career ending at worst. The university in becoming radically secularized—defining reality and making decisions as though God did not exist or matter—has lost its very soul and its contact with the soul of humanity. It has adopted a faith commitment to naturalism where reality is limited to space, time, matter / energy, and nothing else. It has marginalized religious faith and adopted a naturalistic philosophy that ultimately may bring the demise of both religion and science. It marginalizes religion as a superficial storefront to something "more substantive" defined in economic, psychological, or cultural terms. It undermines science by removing any assurance that the universe is ordered, and that we who observe it are capable of being objective (at least in part) in our observations. Jesus, revealed as Logos and Creator, is the key to a unified understanding of life and nature. He alone addresses man's deepest need—reconciliation, (peace) with God, creation, others, and self."

After I finished my remarks, I expected a defensive pushback or even a put down. To my surprise many of them respected what I had to say and shared some of my concerns. There is recognition of the need for a unifying story that would give meaning to the many smaller stories in life. Peace demands such a story, and faith in God is a necessary link to the ultimate story or grand narrative.

Why was and is faith in Jesus marginalized? Jesus' words in John 8:43 explain, "*Why do you not understand what I am saying? It is because you cannot hear My word.*"

Faith is vital to knowledge and wisdom as we read in Hebrews 11:2 *"by faith we understand."* Faith must be integrated into life as a worldview and lifestyle. When Paul spoke of faith that justifies, he is not talking about superficial intellectual ascent to doctrine, simplistic hope in an imaginary myth, or shallow commitment to a generic god. He is speaking of a mind renewing perspective, a life altering commitment, and a rationally grounded hope in Christ. While this faith is not necessary for academic success, the marginalization of its worldview in the academy is a great handicap to full and accurate understanding of man, nature, and history. What does true faith look like? To what extent must saving faith be integrated into one's life in order to be authentic?

Jesus Identifies Abraham's Children

In John 8 we read of an identity crisis as Jesus sizes up the Pharisees while they evaluate him. A critical question is raised in verse 25 where the Jews ask Jesus, "Who are you?" Who was Jesus' father? Was He the Son of God or was He of the devil (verse 48)? The Pharisees claimed to be children of Abraham, but in verse 44 Jesus tells them that their true father is the devil. Why? Because, as Jesus puts it in verse 39, *"If you are Abraham's children, do the deeds of Abraham."* The deeds of Abraham involve "faith" in the Christ, as Paul argues in Romans 4.

Abraham is the "father of faith" and in verse 24 of John 8 Jesus draws attention to this faith, *"for unless you believe that I am He you shall die in your sins."* There are two parts of the Jew's identity crisis in John 8. They wrongly concluded they were sons of Abraham while not believing, and they wrongly concluded they were free from the penalty of sin while sinning. Jesus challenges them on both issues. If they were to respond to Jesus, they must sense their need for liberation from the curse of sin and see their need for faith. True sons of Abraham are convicted sinners who trust Christ as God's provision for sin.

We need both light and sight. If we are blind, we will not see no matter how bright the light might be. While I pray for light in my life, I must also ask for the gift of sight. I remember the first time I saw a "magic eye picture"—one of those multicolored masses of lines that look like a tangled ball of yarn through which a three-dimensional shape emerges if you view it correctly. I stared for nearly thirty minutes at the maze of lines and colors that seemed to make no sense to my brain. Then suddenly the image of a B2 bomber became clear in three-dimensional form. It was so obvious that I was amazed it took so long to see it. For many of us our exposure to the law of God is like a spiritual "magic eye picture." We see the colors and lines, but we just don't get it until that moment of clarity where the image comes into view. We sometimes get all the information, but we refuse to get the message. We see the details but miss the grand narrative. The law was not given to encourage us but to convict us of our need for redemption and to help us identify Jesus as the Redeemer. We must not miss this big picture.

The Sermon on the Mount was a critical challenge to the hard shell of blindness that Satan held over Israel. It also might be said that for many of us today there is blindness to our own sin and need for faith. This is why it is so important to let the law have its say. The terror of the law should develop an appetite for Christ and grace.

John 1:11-13

"11 He came to His own, and those who were His own did not receive Him. 12 But as many as received Him, to them He gave the right to become children of God, {even} to those who believe in His name, 13 who were born not of blood, nor of the will of the flesh, nor of the will of man, but of God." These words help us understand the exchange recorded in John eight. The new birth into God's Kingdom is not determined by ethnic heritage (*"blood"* 1:13) as many of the Jews addressed in John eight believed (*"We*

are Abraham's descendants." 8:33). It is not determined by the *"will of the flesh or of man"* (1:13). That is to say new birth does not originate from us (anything we might will or do "in the flesh"). It is linked to our reception of Jesus as the Christ. This was the one thing the Jews addressed in chapter eight refused to do.

A point to ponder

Our righteousness is Christ,
not our heritage, faith, or moral virtue.

Paul Identifies Abraham's Children

In Romans 4 Paul builds his case for the incompatibility of faith and works by also appealing to Abraham as the father of faith. In chapter 4 verse 5 Paul summarizes his point: *"But to the one who does not work, but believes in Him who justifies the ungodly, his faith is reckoned as righteousness."* The "work" Paul refers to in this passage is associated with "law" and contrasted with "faith." The fact that moral behavior is a part of the "work" is evident in the last part of the verse where God is said to justify the person who is ungodly. God does not give that person the power to win salvation by being good. He declares righteous the one who has not yet been reformed morally. How can God do this? God justifies the sinner because of his faith in Christ who paid the debt of the believer's sins and credited his (Christ's) righteousness to the believer's account.

Paul makes repeated reference to Genesis 15:6, saying, *"And Abraham believed God, and it was reckoned to him as righteousness"* (Rom.4:3, 9, 22). Paul makes a point of the fact that this declaration was made before Abraham had conformed to the demands of the law (including circumcision in Genesis 17:10f). Paul also states that the Gentiles who did not have the law could nonetheless have faith and be justified. This was in keeping with the promise made to Abraham, *"a father of many nations have I made you"* (vs.17). True sons of Abraham are believers even if they do not have the Law.

When it comes to faith, don't confuse means with ends. Let me illustrate. When I was a university student, I lived in a fraternity house with another student who was a Baptist. We would talk about lots of things including our faith. On one occasion he asked me when I had "prayed to receive Christ as my Savior." I told him I was a Lutheran and Lutherans didn't have to do that. "Praying to receive Christ" was something Baptists had to do because they weren't Lutherans. It was hard for him to understand how I could be a Christian without having a dramatic, point-in-time conversion experience. Eventually we both agreed the real issue was "a person's present faith in Christ" not how and when they came to first trust him. It is the ends not the means that are critical.

The Law of Moses was given to bring people to faith in Christ. Abraham's faith came before the tutorial of the law was given, thus demonstrating that faith was possible without the law. Paul's point in Romans 4 and my Baptist friend's reaction illustrate a similar truth: It is easy to confuse the means with the ends. The point of the discussion with my friend is that a living relationship with Christ is the real issue, not how we got there. The point of the covenant with Abraham is faith in God, not hope in the law. While the law intended to lead people to faith, it was not to be equated with faith.

James Identifies Abraham's Children

What is the place of works in the message of grace? How does faithfulness relate to faith? Whenever this question comes up, the second chapter of the book of James is usually sighted. James says, *"faith without works is dead"* (Jas.2:17, 20, 26). But James says something else that is even more challenging to us. In verse 23–24 he says, *"And the Scripture was fulfilled which says, 'and Abraham* *believed God, and it was reckoned to him as righteousness,'* and he was called the friend of God. You see that a man is justified by works, and not by faith alone.*" Isn't this just the opposite of what Paul said in Romans and Galatians?

If we assume the Scriptural texts are not self-contradicting, we must ask ourselves, what does Paul mean and what does James mean? And how do these seemingly opposing views relate? Paul says so much about the subject of justification that it is hard to miss his point. James says relatively little about this subject so we might assume it is James' point that is in most danger of being missed or misunderstood.

There have been many attempted explanations and even expulsions of this text out of respect for Paul's teaching. It would be foolish to assume I have the only or best answer when great minds and hearts have labored with the tension between Paul and James. Luther was quite right in sensing the gravity of the apparent stress created by James' teaching on the gospel message of grace.

As I have wrestled with this dilemma, there are two observations that have guided my understanding. First, James 2 was probably written before Galatians, and I believe is best understood as a practical manual for following Christ. I take my cue from verse 14 and the phrase, *"what use is it?"* This passage is addressing the usefulness of faith, especially in the affairs of this life. For example, look at verses 15–16: *"If a brother or sister is without clothing and in need of daily food, and one of you says to them, 'Go in peace, be warmed and be filled,' and yet you do not give them what is necessary for their body, what use is that?"* And again, *"I will show you my faith by my works"* (Jas.2:18). James is concerned about the demonstration of faith before his fellow men and in the context of living in this world.

Second, it is very likely that James uses the words "justification" and "faith" in ways that are different from the way Paul uses them. It is entirely possible that the "justification" James has in mind is not the Pauline concept of man's relationship with God, but rather man's relationships in this world before man. In other words, authentic faith is "fulfilled" or demonstrated in actions that other people can see. In Romans 4:2 Paul says, *"For if Abraham was justified by works, he has something to boast about; but not before God."* Abraham's works might mean something before man but are not necessary before God. God sees the heart, but man only sees the actions. Abraham was justified before God when he believed apart from any obedience to the law of God. Abraham was justified before his fellow man only when he demonstrated his faith in ways man could see.

Paul like James seemed to believe works justified him *in the eyes of men*. To answer his critics Paul did not talk of his faith but of his works. We see vivid examples of this in 1 Thessalonians 2:3–10 and 2 Corinthians 11:18–28. Paul warned Titus about "those of the circumcision" saying, *"They profess to know God, but by their deeds they deny Him..."* (Tit.1:16). He spoke of the *"work of faith"* in 1 Thessalonians 1:3 and 2 Thessalonians 1:11. He observed, *"faith works through love"* (Gal.5:6). While Paul championed justification before God through faith apart from human moral virtue, he also recognizes that saving faith is expected to produce virtue for man to see.

The willingness of Abraham to sacrifice his son is the most dramatic example of faith in action and perhaps that is why James uses it (Gen.22) in James 2:21. For Paul in Romans 4:9–10, the justification of Abraham by faith is a declaration by God that takes place long before Abraham's works of faithfulness (in this case circumcision and/or the offering of Isaac) and that is why Paul uses this example. For Paul justification has to do with Abraham's standing before God, not his standing before man. So we might say Abraham was justified (declared righteous before God) when Abraham believed God—and long before he obeyed the law of God. But it is also true to say that Abraham, as a man of faith, was justified by fulfilling his faith—bearing fruit of faith *in his conduct* before others.

In what sense does this faith in action "save him" (Jas.2:14)? The most common use of the Greek word for "save" in the Bible is of a temporal material deliverance, not an eternal spiritual salvation. An example of this is seen in James 5:15. *"The prayer offered in faith will save the one who is sick, and the Lord will raise him up."* The salvation of the temporal life is in view here. This temporal context may be what James has in mind in chapter two. We are saved from uselessness (Jas.2:4,16,20) through good works motivated by faith.

We must also draw a distinction between faith as confession without a conviction and faith rooted in repentance. There is no virtue in an orthodox confession without deep personal conviction. The initial fruits of true faith (repentance from dead works and hope in Christ) include calling on Jesus as Lord, water baptism, and open identification with Christ's church. Saving faith will over time lead to turning from sins, a desire to follow Jesus as Lord, and selfless service to others. The same faith that justifies the believer before God inwardly justifies the believer before others outwardly. The first justification is apart from any moral merit while the second is by open moral virtue.

True Faith

Justifies before God	Justifies before man
(Paul)	(James)
Inward conviction	Outward conduct
Saves (the spirit)	Saves (the body)

James and Paul do not disagree. They do not represent two different traditions or theologies. They

137

address the issue of faith and works from two different contexts as summarized in the above chart.

My first job interview after finishing my university studies was with a landscape architectural firm in Dallas, Texas. With a landscape architecture degree under my belt, I was eager to use my training. In the interview the head of the firm asked to see some of my work. I told her I did not have job experience only a BS degree. Her response was, "Can you draft?" My reply was, "Anyone can draft; I have been trained to design." She said, "Before I will give you a job, I need to see what you can do. You must start by learning to be a good draftsman." She knew my degree did not mean much if I could not do the most basic work, and the only way to know if I had the goods was to let me show her. Little did I know she had much more to show me about real-life demands of landscape design than I had to show her about my talent as a designer. It would be a full year before I was given serious design responsibilities.

James is approaching faith in a practical not theoretical way. He is saying, "Show me. I can't accept as real what I can't verify through actions." It is not only what you claim to know; it is also what you are able to demonstrate. The person offering me a job rightly demanded to see me do some work before giving me design responsibilities.

Abraham's Children have a Special Trust in God

I hope we now see the link between imputed righteousness and faith, but do we have the kind of faith that brings imputed righteousness? How can we distinguish between living and dead faith? To be justified before God, how much faith is needed? How does one acquire saving faith?

First, we will identify different kinds of faith. There is faith that is common to all people. It includes a commonsense trust that is necessary to get on in the world. I believe the sun will come up in the morning and go down again at night. There is also a worldview or faith assumption concerning how life works—science, religion, etc. Everyone operates with some overall assumption about how the world works. We also trust other individuals in specific circumstances as we live our lives. For example, I can trust the local police to respect and enforce the laws.

When the Bible talks about faith, it uses the word in a different way. The Bible talks about "faith as orthodox doctrine", as an objective, religious confession and subjective religious experience shared by a community. For example, we speak of being true to "the faith." This might be a form of worldview faith. Coupled with orthodox belief but distinct from it is tactical faith. It includes trusting God for specifics. For example, I may trust that God will guide my steps. This is not saving faith but practical living faith.

Saving faith is commitment to God as Redeemer Lord through His Son Jesus. It is a confession of Christ based on a conviction that He died and rose for my eternal life. It is this last type of faith we set our focus on. Not that it can or should be completely divorced from "the faith" or "living by faith." As we have seen saving faith is expressed through dynamic faith and commitment to "the faith." We might say saving faith encompasses all of the above types of faith and comes with an installation of Christ's Spirit into our hearts as we are placed "in Christ." Note the following chart.

General faith	Biblical faith
Formal Worldview – materialism, theism, etc.	**Body of Doctrine** – "the faith"
Social expectations – trusting another person	**Tactical** – "trusting God to answer prayer"
Common sense – the sun will rise in the morning	**Saving faith** – "eternal life"

Is it Possible to have Real
Saving Faith and be Disobedient?

While we expect those who confess faith to also show it, we know in the case of the Corinthian church, for example, there were many true "*saints*" who acted like "*mere men*" or people of the world (1 Cor.3:3). This is not to say these Corinthians had no fruit in their lives. They were alive to God in many ways while being blind to the kingdom in some inexcusable areas. We can and often do have the same experience. Christians are not perfect, but if they have authentic saving faith, they have experienced a change of direction in their hearts (inner lives) even if not obvious to anyone but God.

We must never forget that the New Testament letters were written to congregations of believers who were sinners in need of correction. Whenever someone makes a reference to the New Testament church as a model for the modern church, I want to ask, "Which New Testament church do you have in mind?" Could it be the church at Ephesus with its racism, or the churches in Galatia with their legalism, or the church in Thessalonica with its misplaced prophetic understanding? Maybe it was Corinth you had in mind? I doubt it. The church has always been a work in progress, and that will continue. The same can be said for each of us personally.

I have fond memories of teaching in an inner city African American community in the greater Dallas area. On one occasion the subject of personal holiness came up. One of the women in the class announced she had reached perfection in her life. An elderly man across the room asked that we verify her claim with her husband. Everyone roared with laughter because they knew claims of holiness are easy to make in the presence of those who don't have to live with us. In all fairness most people who claim "complete sanctification" are referring to the total consecration of their heart to obey God. They are not saying they are perfect in word and deed. But even claims of perfection in motive and intent are suspect from my experience. I remember one of the elders in our congregation confessing that he was thankful his motives were "at least" mixed, as that was a considerable step up from where they were before he came to understand God's grace. Our motives like our actions are not the source of our righteousness. Our righteousness is Christ.

Trust Should Lead to Obedience.

When someone confessing faith does not display any interest in following Christ, there are reasons to question the integrity of his or her confession. Has that person ever really come to Christ? Have they experienced Christ's Spirit so as to come alive spiritually—perhaps not?

We see Abraham's life of faith in (Rom.4:17–25) as an example of conduct motivated by trust. The faith that justifies is a growing confidence that because Christ was raised from the dead, my sins are forgiven and I will one day be raised with Him. Abraham believed God could bring life from Sarah's dead womb and from Isaac's sacrificed body. Faith that justifies will grow through testing. Abraham was asked to wait and be willing to give back to God that which God had promised him in his son Isaac. Faith that justifies will lead to obedience. As James points out to us, Abraham's faith was fully developed as he obeyed. Faith that justifies will submit to water baptism. Abraham was obedient in identifying himself through circumcision with the covenant promise of God. Faith that justifies is alive to God in spite of human weakness. Abraham's weakness did not stop him from trusting God.

The relationship of saving faith and faithfulness to the law is both controversial and critical to a proper understanding of radical grace and peace. At the center of the controversy are two concerns. One is the concern that the radical nature of God's grace be recognized, and the second is that the authenticity of genuine repentance and the new birth be respected. Some have so fought to preserve one that they have endangered the integrity of the other.

For example, it is possible to speak of radical grace and say little or nothing about moral responsibility for fear of introducing salvation by discipleship or moral merit. Some seem to ignore the fact that there are many moral imperatives for Christians in Paul's letters, and yet some pretend Paul's letters are just written in the indicative mood. That is to say we should only concentrate on our new identity under grace and not talk about moral obligations that sound like "law." One of the signs of Christ's indwelling Spirit is a moral tension that prevents the believer from being given over fully to the flesh with its lusts (Rom.8:1-17, Eph.2:1-10, Gal.5:16-26).

On the other hand it is also possible to so emphasize the imperatives of the New Testament that the authentic motivation of grace is lost, and we are left thinking and behaving like modern day Pharisees, consumed with our duties, controlled by our fears, and condemned to guilt or pride by our conduct.

A point to ponder

Trust God to answer your prayers
and also to make you an answer
to someone else's prayers.

Look at the Christian's life as a plant. A normal healthy plant will grow, bear leaves, reproduce, and give other signs of life. It is possible however for a plant to be very much alive in the root but look dead above ground. By all appearances the plant may appear to have no life in its branches, but if we could look beneath the surface we would see there is indeed life present. This is like the person who is justified before God but not before man.

Every true Christian will bear fruit from the indwelling life of Christ. But much of that fruit may be hidden from the view of others. This inconspicuous fruitfulness is not the norm but it nonetheless exists. The same analogy can be made of the human body. We might be inclined to say if someone is unconscious, not breathing, and without a pulse, they are dead. But we know of people who have been revived from such conditions. When CPR is successfully performed, we do not claim to have raised someone from the dead. We realize life was still present, but it was not evident. In some cases only the great physician knows. So it is with some Christians.

Another analogy I find useful is marriage. We might look at the coming together of a man and a woman in marriage as sharing a common life. The notion of a confession of faith and no fellowship or sharing in the life of Christ is as strange as a marriage ceremony with the couple then going their separate ways. It is unusual and unnatural. But as we know, a married couple can act as though they are not married for a period of time.

Faith Confessions May Not Last.

If a person makes an honest confession of faith, can they lose that faith? Of course they can. It happens all too often. We are secure on the basis of a present living faith not a past faith. It makes no difference how sincere a previous confession may have been. If the faith is not a present living reality, there is no ground for security. Now we can debate all day long as to whether or not the original confession was true faith or wishful thinking, but the fact remains some people who were at one point in their own minds sincere believers no longer confess faith in Christ. That fact is not open to debate. But it is not the sin of moral failure that results in the loss of salvation; it is the sin of unbelief. Note: Rom.11:17–23; Col.1:21–23; Gal.5:4.

If you believe you can sin to the point of losing your salvation, let me ask you this question: "How serious

143

a sin do you have to commit to lose God's grace?" Will you lose God's grace if you commit murder and adultery like King David, blasphemy like Peter, and continue in a state of "knowing what is right yet not doing it" like Paul? The problem with sin disqualifying us from God's grace is that we didn't and couldn't deserve salvation to start with. How can we lose it if we still don't deserve it? Only Pharisees think they have become good enough to not need grace. The rest of us need massive doses daily not just for unconscious ethical slips but also for intentional, first-degree (premeditated) sins of active rebellion.

To be sure true saving faith is more than intellectual assent, emotional experience, verbal confession of truth, and ceremonial acts. True saving faith is a deep repentance, a changing of one's mind toward Christ. This repentance will be life changing. It is this subject of repentance we will explore in the second book in this series *Peace Makers*.

Questions for Application and Discussion

1. How do you know you have true faith?
2. Are there limits to the kinds of disobedience true faith will tolerate?
3. How did you come to faith in Christ?
4. What is the object and content of true saving faith?
5. How would you summarize the message of this chapter?
6. Are there parts of this chapter with which you disagree? Why?

Chapter 9
Satan – The Father of Misplaced Hope

Obstacle #3 to Peace with God:
An Independent Spirit

To experience peace with God, we must
stop believing the lies of Satan.

Humans are naturally creatures of faith. We all have faith in something or someone. The question is what do we trust? Faith can be centered in a philosophy (like materialism), religious rituals (like baptism), spiritual disciplines (like prayer), or institutions (like the church); but it will exist. Will faith in these things justify us before God or bring us the kind of peace we seek and need? Such faith is not saving faith. Our faith may be real enough, but if its object is unworthy of ultimate trust, it will be little more than raw idolatry. Without faith it is impossible to please God, but not all faith pleases God.

A friend of mine who is very sensitive to the whole realm of "spiritual warfare" asked if I would teach a class on the subject. I was glad to do so, but I warned her it would not be anything like what she expected. It would not deal with exorcizing demons, separating oneself from defiling books, places, and people, or praying a hedge of angelic protection around our families while we isolated ourselves from the broader culture. I started by reminding the class that Satan as a fallen angel is like all angels. He is a messenger—the father of lies. He works primarily in the world of thoughts, ideas, perceptions, expectations, and hopes—false hopes. I illustrated this point with examples of Satan's confrontation with Eve in Genesis 3 and Jesus in Matthew 4 where the temptation was to live life independent of faith in God. I suggested that in Western culture Satan is trying to do the same thing as he pushes our world and life view in a secular direction. Secularism relegates Christian faith to a private experience divorced from much of life. In a secular society God becomes practically irrelevant. Secularism shifts faith to self, leaders, science, technology, etc.—anything but Christ.

A point to ponder

Satan will promote hope in anything
and everything but Christ.

So what is Satan's lie? I am coming to believe it boils down to one word—independence. In our culture we declare our independence from all external authority. We segregate culture from God. We segregate our lives from faith. We celebrate a figurehead Messiah (Jesus) on Sunday while placing our true hope in the things of this world during the week. Sometimes this independence is disguised when we use God to help us reach our temporal material goal. For example, why do so many of our prayer requests focus on getting and keeping temporal material things— finances, physical health, etc. Jesus is treated like our cosmic servant—ready and waiting to assist us in reaching the "American dream." We tend to define reality and make decisions as though God does not exist or matter until we need a crutch or gift. We find our hope in anything and everything but God.

A great obstacle to peace with God is the lie of a false hope. It is possible to have false assurance or security—a false sense of being in a "right relationship with God." Jesus addresses this exact problem in John 8 where he describes Satan as the father of lies (Jn.8:44). Paul speaks of the spirit of lawlessness that will characterize the antichrist spirit of the last days (2 Thess.2:6–9). James makes it clear that even the demons believe in God, (Jas.2:19), but that does not change their character. It is also possible to have real faith in the real God but to have our expectations of God distorted by

146

Satan. How many sincere Christians have prayed in faith only to be left confused, cynical, or bitter when their expectations were unrealized.

Satan's Strategy is to Center our Hope in Anything and Everything but Christ.

I am convinced Satan has a vested interest not in destroying our hope but in building our hope in anything and everything *but* God's grace in Christ. We have two dramatic accounts of Satan's temptations. One is of Eve in Genesis 3. In this passage we read of the serpent's lie to Eve concerning the true object of her hope. He tells her if she takes seriously the word of God, she will not realize her potential; but if she relies on her independent judgment, she will gain the knowledge that "is key" to happiness.

Satan was partly right in that Eve (and we who are her descendants) did gain knowledge, but it did not lead to happiness because it was divorced from wisdom and faith. Knowledge, without God, leaves the soul empty. Children of Satan are those who are ever increasing in knowledge but not in wisdom. Many of the Jews of Jesus' time were in that number as are many of us.

The second dramatic account of Satan's activity is found in Matthew chapter four where Satan tempts Jesus. On three occasions Satan comes to Christ with a strategy to dislodge him from the Kingdom's hope and to fix his hope on temporal cultural perspectives and his own efforts. This suggests that at the root of our anxiety, guilt, fear, and anger, is a rebellious resistance to trusting God. Going on our own, we choose to find hope in other things—family, marriage, vocation, church, personal abilities, etc. In so doing we become children of Satan.

The Offense of Jesus to a Postmodern World

The Word of the Cross—the Gospel is a stumbling block and rock of offense on several grounds. Blood sacrifice insults modern culture's sense of civility. The idea that

God's wrath is satisfied at the cross insults our sense of God's loving character. Substitutionary atonement insults our sense of personal moral merit. Dying with Christ in baptism insults our autonomy and right to realize our dreams. But there is no greater offense to our modern mind than the idea of an exclusive salvation, which insults our sense of fairness.

The spiritual leaders of Jesus' day were not offended by exclusive religious beliefs per say. It was Jesus' claims concerning himself that offended. Jesus had the audacity to suggest he was the only worthy object of faith because faith in him was the same as faith in God. Today our culture does not seem to object to Jesus' claim to be the Son of God so long as His claim does not imply he is the only way to God or the only Son of God. One prominent theologian put it this way when asked if he believed in the deity of Jesus: "I have never denied the deity of Jesus. As a matter of fact, I have never denied the deity of any human."

A point to ponder

**Satan feels no threat from faith.
It's faith in Jesus as Lord
that he resists.**

One of the first tests for credibility that our popular culture gives to any religion (including Christianity) is expressed in the question: Is this system exclusive? If so, culture shuns it in the name of pluralism. In modern Western culture the whole idea of exclusion on the basis of Christian faith has been scorned as imperialistic. If God is loving, powerful, and fair, surely there must be hope for those who live relatively moral lives with noble intentions but have rejected the Christian Gospel. The idea of an elite kingdom requiring narrow and restricted beliefs excluding all who do not confess faith in Christ sounds like spiritual snobbery. We are told if this narrow-minded image is the true Christ of the gospel story, he is not worthy of respect. He should be scorned or at least marginalized.

The Grace of God is More Exclusive than Many Want to Believe.

Our pluralistic culture has presented many challenges to the traditional Christian view of faith. One popular lie of Satan is to separate God's love from Christ's sacrifice. We are prompted to ask: Is it possible that God's grace is broader than many of us have assumed? Is it possible that God's saving grace is extended to sincere people of faith in God who have never heard the name Jesus or who adhere to other religious traditions? Much of the impulse behind this question comes from a Christian paradox: God's love for all people vs. the exclusiveness of the Christian view of salvation.

Is it true that only a small remnant (the elect) will be saved through calling on the name of Christ Jesus in faith? All others will be damned no matter what their circumstances or faith traditions. This exclusive view has become the traditional position following Augustine, Luther, and Calvin. Augustine put it bluntly: "There is no doubt that not only all the heathen, but also all Jews and all heretics and schismatics who die outside the church will go into that everlasting fire prepared for the devil and his angels." Luther added: "Those who remain outside Christianity, be they heathens, Turks, Jews or false Christians (Roman Catholics), although they believe on only one true God yet remain in eternal wrath and perdition."

There is little question that millions of people have a living faith in "God" but not in Jesus Christ. This has raised some difficult questions for Christians. Is it really fair for God to harshly judge those who have not even heard the gospel? What about those who have a sincere trust in God as their Lord but are not Christians? How does

God relate to them? While many of these questions go unanswered, we can say this: Any serious reading of the Bible and any survey of church history will force one to conclude that the Christian faith as expressed in Scripture and history is exclusive. There are some people who are sincere, even zealous in their faith, but lost in their sins and destined for judgment.

In Romans 10:1–3 Paul writes, *"Brethren, my heart's desire and my prayer to God for them is for their salvation. For I bear them witness that they have a zeal for God, but not in accordance with knowledge. For not knowing about God's righteousness, and seeking to establish their own, they did not subject themselves to the righteousness of God."* Observe the following characteristics of those for whom Paul is so concerned. First, Paul is concerned for their salvation. Apparently they are not included in the community of the saved. Second, they have zeal in their faith, and their zeal is for the one true God. It is not as though they were not committed to God. Third, they were uninformed of the grace of the gospel. They had not known about the grace of God in Christ, yet this did not excuse them. It is difficult to avoid the obvious fact that in spite of their zeal for God and their lack of exposure to the gospel, they are lost. I am not suggesting this passage settles the issue of God's relationship with those who have never heard or those who believe God but are not confessing Christians. But I am saying this: It is very difficult to make the Christian faith politically correct and still be faithful to the biblical record.

One of the most difficult challenges in ministering within a politically correct community is the presentation of the true gospel without losing the audience over the exclusiveness clause. If you say only those who have "your kind of faith" in God will go to heaven, you are dismissed as a fundamentalist bigot. If you say Christianity is not exclusive, you are a heretic. Is there a way to communicate the biblical gospel without being dismissed as a bigot or a heretic?

At one point I was asked to speak to a university audience I knew would expect me to offend them with an exclusive Gospel. When the question came up, I told the story of the Gospel with eight points.

1. I am not called to judge who goes to heaven or hell. I am called to proclaim good news to sinners.

2. God will judge all people with complete fairness. Differences of religion, race, ethnicity, intelligence, sex, and so on will not distort God's objectivity.

3. The basis of God's judgment will be His own character and our conformity to it as those created in and called to bear His image. In a sense we might say God simply expects us to be true to ourselves as humans designed to reflect the image of our Creator.

4. The sobering news is that God will not be grading on the curve and that makes some of us nervous.

5. The good news is that God has given His Son as a substitute for those who feel insecure and unworthy to stand before God clothed only in their own righteousness or lack thereof.

6. Many of us are so painfully aware of our spiritual and social failures that we are thrilled to know of God's gift of grace, and we have accepted it.

7. But if this is not your choice, do not for a moment think we are saying God will be unfair with you. He will be fair in judging you on the basis of your moral record.

8. The ball is in your court. You do not have to place your faith in Christ, but you will have to face a God who has created you to reflect His image. You can stand before God without Christ if you wish.

These points do not answer all the questions, but they put the emphasis in the right place—God's gift and our choice.

The Grace of God is Less Exclusive than Many Believe.

There is another extreme that stands in stark contrast to universalism's "faith." Attachment to the "Christian community" is sometimes defined in such detail that only those of a particular sect qualify. At this point one must wonder if faith is to be centered in the gospel, or is it centered in the numerous doctrines of a specific sect of Christianity? In some circles if a person does not honor the Saturday Sabbath law, they are not truly Christian. Others have made an issue of the wording used at one's baptism suggesting only those baptized within "their sect" are forgiven of their sins. Others have suggested that the object of faith is the church, or the leadership, or a particular social tradition. The point is this: Just as it is possible to extend our hope to include virtually everyone in God's redeemed family, so it is possible to exclude nearly everyone who is not just like us.

Satan's Lies

Consider the condition of the Jewish leaders who were identified by Jesus as *"of your father the devil"* (Jn.8:44). How did they see themselves? Or more importantly what were the lies they had believed about true faith? We know they found great security in their national heritage. They felt that the blood descendents of Abraham were given special status with God. They also prided themselves in being recipients of special revelation (the law), which gave them special knowledge about God and His ways. They found comfort in their moral discipline with respect to the demands of the law. They fell for the lies of spiritual security through superficial position and privilege rather than genuine, heartfelt faith.

Here are some of Satan's more common lies in our own modern-day setting. Note that these deceptions are in some ways similar to Israel's misunderstandings. First, many people believe that general faith in God (whoever he, she, or it may be) is all that is necessary. Anything more specific runs the risk of offending someone. Some people may call this kind of faith "civil religion" (a faith that sees God as a chaplain to the general culture's interests).

Another lie is the idea that "Christian morality or social service" is the essence of Christian faith. This is the popular notion, which says that being a Christian has less to do with beliefs than it does with behaviors. Many would say a Christian is anyone who generally follows the ethical teaching of Jesus. Are personal and social ethics the outward fruit of true faith or the essence of it?

For some people Christianity is simply a matter of affiliation. Does affiliation with a Christian church or even growing up in a Christian family automatically make a person a true believer?

Another common lie identifies Christian faith with a religious experience of some kind. Feeling the presence of something that can only be described as a spiritual force may have nothing to do with Christ. The fact that such a feeling may have been experienced in a church or at a Christian meeting may not in itself mean anything. Even being baptized in water does not automatically make a person a Christian. We must here note that genuine faith is not just a public confession or intellectual ascent to a system of teaching. While each of these experiences may be an authentic expression of true faith, they are not in and of themselves guarantees of faith.

We are Not Saved by Faith, Hope, and Love.

Perhaps the greatest lie of Satan is that the object of our faith should be faith, hope, and love. If you just believe in something, anything, and if you have hope of eternal bliss, and if you love your fellowman, you are okay with "God." Such perspectives suggest the real call is to belief in a generic god and commitment to love your fellowman. Some believe that those who love others, whatever that means, will be welcomed into God's presence at the end. Doctrines about God or gods and about atonement and

153

Jesus as the only way are unnecessary and even confusing to those who fall for this falsehood. Just have faith, hope, and love. While this lie may be popular and widespread, it is still a lie. The biblical gospel is exclusive, and those who reject it as primitive and unjust are siding with their father Satan according to Jesus in John 8. The N.T. letters indicate that the Apostles were obsessed with Jesus, but it was not his ethical teaching that defined their message. It was faith in the finished work of the cross and the resurrection that defined the Gospel 1 Cor.15:1-5). This was because the basic issue in peace (with ourselves, others, and God) is holiness through personal merit or through holiness imputed in Christ.

What is Genuine Saving Faith?

Genuine Christian faith is best described as a transfer of hope for reconciliation with God (from something other than Christ) to Christ. True Christian faith means receiving Jesus as one's personal surrogate on the cross so that we die with him. Our life and hope are tied to Jesus. When the focus of our hope changes, so will the focus of our life. Christian faith involves a commitment to change the direction of our lives so we might seek and follow the teachings and life of Christ as Lord and God. Mature faith is rooted in the Gospel that is intellectually convincing, emotionally satisfying, culturally inspiring, socially connecting, and morally transforming.

In the previous chapter I used marriage as an illustration. I will expand the analogy here. The marriage commitment might be viewed in three stages. First, there is what we might call "courtship." This is the stage where commitment is sought and often secured through a rather complex process of social, emotional, and intellectual negotiations. The second stage is "commitment." This is where we make a decision to share our life with another. The third stage we call "ceremony." This is the official wedding where the courtship leads to commitment that is made public and official. In many ways the wedding is viewed as the point of commitment even though the real commitment may have been made informally some time before the ceremony. The fourth stage we call "communion." This is where the commitment that grew out of courtship and was officially sanctioned at the wedding ceremony is lived out as both husband and wife share their lives together.

Christian faith follows a similar path. There is a stage where the Spirit of Christ courts us. We might call this evangelism. It is during this stage that we wrestle with the emotional, social, and intellectual elements of commitment. We eventually come to a place where we are willing to place our faith in what we know, see, and feel. To receive Christ by faith we personally commit our lives to him. The third stage is water baptism. Baptism is the "marriage ceremony" of faith where we are officially joined to Christ. It is not where faith is created but where faith is expressed publicly. It is where we identify the beginning of our official walk with Christ. The fourth stage is the communion or commingling of our life and Christ's life. Some people have referred to this stage as the installation of Christ's Spirit into our everyday life. It is the process of living out our new life "in Christ." It is where the fruit of our commitment is most fully expressed.

> ### *A point to ponder*
>
> The normal Christian life
> provides for but does not require
> perfect faithfulness.

It is natural for a married couple to live their lives in intimate communion. It is expected that people who make a profession of faith no longer live for themselves. But the selfless union once pledged at the marriage ceremony is seldom followed perfectly. The same can be said for a person's commitment to Christ. Some believers are more faithful than others. There are times when a believer's fidelity is strong and times when it is weak. While it is technically possible for a couple to be married and never share their lives, this would be unnatural and quite unusual. We can say the same thing about those who profess Christian faith. Satan lies when he accuses us of false faith every time we fail to live out our faith perfectly. By the same token he also lies when he tells us we have genuine faith when we have gone through the ceremony but never really committed our lives to walk after Christ, or have never really submitted our lives to the rule of Christ's Spirit in our lives. If we live by the Spirit, we will be led by the Spirit and will walk (though not perfectly) by the Spirit.

Questions for Application and Discussion

1. What do you believe to be the most common example of false faith?

2. How would you respond to a confessing Christian who was living in open disrespect and disobedience to his or her faith?

3. Have you ever had serious doubts about your relationship with God? What, if anything, has helped you deal with the doubts?

4. How would you summarize the message of this chapter?

5. What parts of the chapter do you find hardest to buy? Why?

6. What do you sense are the most damaging "false messages" that Satan sows in our culture?

Conclusion

The Gospel of Grace and Peace

Personal inner peace is a spiritual issue that ultimately does not depend on our outer circumstances or our inner virtue. It is a gift of God's grace that we learn through hearing the Gospel story. This story is applied to our lives as we receive by faith the good news of two great imputations. It is the great exchange where our sins are imputed to Christ and Christ's righteousness is imputed to those who believe. In the same way and to the same extent that Christ bore our sins, so we bear his righteousness. As he who knew no sin became sinful for us, so we who remain imperfect are declared righteous as we are united with Christ by faith. This grace is not cheap. Its price is the death of the only begotten Son of God. This grace is a legal fact based on a New Covenant in Christ's blood. It is not automatically applied to everyone but must be received by faith in keeping with the true children of Abraham.

God is looking for a Certain Type of Person.

God is not looking for disciples who have life under successful management, who are well bred, polished, gifted, and charming. No! He seeks dirty, rotten sinners who are broken and desperate. They will know and express the grace of God in a way that will bring rest to the soul and peace to this world. They will be peace seekers and will become peacemakers.

Tommy grew up in a conservative Christian home where he and his friends could be found in church every Sunday and on the right side of the tracks every week. He was smart, attractive, gifted, popular, and proud. But deep inside was a sense of shame inherited from a legalistic religious culture and a sensitive soul made in the image of God. After an outstanding athletic career in high school and college, he entered a graduate program at a premier university,

157

which he finished with honors. He married his high school sweetheart, started a family, and set out on what promised to be a stellar career in medicine.

Fast-forward twenty years—Tommy is alone in a prison cell, curled in a fetal position contemplating suicide. He has lost his wife, family, career, reputation, dignity, and pride. It was while imprisoned for forgery because of an addiction to pain killers that Tommy looked through the window of his brokenness and saw the grace of God. Earlier in his life Tommy would drive by the state prison and think, "what a sad group of losers these prisoners must be." Little did he realize that one day he would find himself behind that razor wire fence, a broken soul.

Fast-forward again—while sitting in my living room with tears in his eyes, Tommy tells me that he is leaving eleven years of incarceration with more than he had when he went in. He had lost nearly everything when he entered prison. Even his physical life was threatened at the hands of another inmate. And now he was facing the world as a convicted felon. Yet it was at the very point of total and complete brokenness that the greatest treasure of life was found. Tommy encountered the grace of God in the face of a fellow inmate serving life on a murder charge. It was when this convicted murderer with compassion shared a pair of shoes with Tommy that he saw a ray of hope that eventually became a burst of spiritual sunrise in his life. For years grace was just another doctrine in Tommy's life—a life dominated by both inner shame and outer pride. As a broken person in a broken world, Tommy found God's perfect peace and so can you. I am reminded of the words of another prisoner who wrote, "Grace to you and peace from God our Father and the Lord Jesus Christ." (Phil.1:2) "I count all things to be loss in view of the surpassing value of knowing Christ Jesus my Lord, for whom I have suffered the loss of all things" (Phil.3:8).

The Message of this Book in a Nut Shell

The argument of this book can be summarized by drawing attention to three steps to strategic peace with God.

Step #1 The **Spirit of Holiness** - taking seriously Jesus' words about personal holiness and being broken by them.

Step #2 The **Spirit of a New Covenant** - moving our eye away from what we could not do to what God has done for us in Christ.

Step #3 The **Spirit of Faith** - receiving the free gift of Christ's righteousness available to us through faith. It is a righteousness that is *for* us and then works *in* and *through* us.

There are also three obstacles to peace with God.

Obstacle #1 A **Lawless Spirit** - building a foundation of self-sufficiency that does not understand the just demands of a holy God.

Obstacle #2 A **Legalistic Spirit** - inviting us to live under the Law of Moses will keep us anxious, bitter, or proud.

Obstacle #3 An **Independent Spirit** - looking for hope in anything and everything but God.

Peace Seekers is the first of two books. The second, *Peace Makers,* continues to explore the grace of God as it enables us to be peacemakers by transforming our posture toward our work, our moral behavior, and our relationships.

A Final Note

The thesis of *Peace Seekers* may raise questions in the minds of those who are students of the Bible. There are a number of passages that seem to convey a different message than the radical grace that I have outlined in this book. In the Appendix that follows I have offered a response to over forty Biblical passages that seem to challenge the radical grace that I am teaching. A second book *Peace Makers* will also clarify some common concerns as it develops the social implications of grace and peace. It looks at grace and worship, grace and repentance, and finally grace and faithfulness. In an Appendix it also addresses commonly asked questions about law and grace as they relate to the Christian life. It also will address the question of "Discipleship Salvation," or does a person have to be a Christ follower in every area of their life to be a "born again" Christian.

Appendix #1
Some Troubling Passages with Respect to Radical Grace

A Great Controversy

It may come as no surprise that not everyone is in agreement with the biblical teaching on radical grace. The reason for differing understandings of God's grace come not from a lack of exposure to the Bible. Many of those who are debating the relationship of law to grace are devout Christians who are serious students of the Scripture.

Nearly everyone who reads the Old Testament and New Testament is made aware of the tension within Scripture between the law of God demanding performance from man with appropriate rewards and punishment following, and the grace of God, which rewards and accepts the believer unconditionally. This tension is sensed in the relationship between the Synoptic Gospels and the Epistles of the New Testament.

Even the statements of Paul on the subject of law often appear to be contradictory or at least confusing. For example, consider the following issues.

- Have Christians died to the law, and are they free from it (Rom.6:14, 7:1–6, Gal.2:19, 5:1); or do they uphold the law and fulfill it (Rom.3:31, 8:4, 13:8–10, Gal.5:14)?

- Is the law contrary to faith and Christ (Rom.2–4, 2 Cor.3, Gal.3–4), or is it of faith (Rom.3:27) or of Christ (1 Cor.9:21, Gal.6:2)?

- Is justification apart from works of the law (Rom.3:20, Gal.2:16, 5:4), or is it by works (Rom.2:1–16, 2 Cor.5:10, Gal.6:4–8)?

- When circumcision is commanded of God in the Old Testament, how can Paul tell the Corinthians it does not matter if they are not circumcised so long as they keep the commandments of God (1 Cor.7:19)?

- If the law is the "holy law of God" (Rom.7:10–14, 9:4), how could Paul regard it as responsible for sin, curses, and death (Rom.7:5, 2 Cor.3:6–9, Gal.3:10–13)?

The confusion and crisis within the early church over the relationship of the Gentile believers to the Jewish church as expressed in Acts 15 is another example of the tension between law and grace. This tension, we might add, is still present in the church today.

The Epistle of James and the letters of Paul (especially Galatians and Romans) have left many people confused. Do Paul and James really belong in the same theological family? Luther for one felt James was an outsider to orthodoxy. We see this tension expressed most dramatically in James 2:14–26 when compared to Romans 4:1–25 and Galatians 3:1–14.

We might summarize the tension by looking at two different interpretations of Romans 10:4, "*For Christ is the end of the law for righteousness to everyone who believes.*" Is the Greek word "*end*" to be understood as 1) fulfilled so as to terminate (Matt.1:22; 2:15,17,23; 3:15; 4:14; 8:17) or 2) confirm and install (Rom.15:19; 2 Cor.10:6; Jas.2:23)? Which of these equally possible understandings is correct? Did Jesus perfectly illustrate or exemplify the Law of Moses, or did he satisfy its demands so as to terminate it as a force and standard by which people would be judged?

The practical implications of this issue are widespread and deep. Does "grace" mean I am acceptable to God apart from my performance, or is the "fine print" legalistic? How am I, as a Christian, to apply the Old Testament law's ceremonial, dietary, and Sabbath demands? Is it proper to use Old Covenant worship structures (altar, priest, temple, sacrifice, confession of sins, etc.) in a New Covenant context?

Biblical scholars have tried to resolve these tensions in different ways. One solution comes from a radical historical critical approach to the biblical text. This approach does not expect the Scripture to be internally consistent because it is believed to be the work of man not God. Those who take this position have concluded that the biblical material represents several diverse theologies and is hopelessly inconsistent. They assume the biblical texts evolved over time and were primarily the product of historical, cultural, and political forces that we will never fully understand. This is not really a solution but rather an explanation of a hopeless internal contradiction within the Bible. Those who hold this view would insist that any "harmonization" of law and grace would be forced and fail to take seriously the texts of the Bible, which are understood as products of natural, evolving, and differing ideas. Such a response is not an attractive option for those who read the Bible with the assumption that its divinely inspired message is internally consistent.

Some have emphasized the continuity between the Old Covenant law and New Covenant's emphasis on the gracious ministry of the Holy Spirit (Matt.5:17–19, Mk.7:1–23, Rom.7:12,14,22, 1 Tim.1:8). This usually involves toning down the harshness of Paul's criticism of "the law" and drawing attention to the grace within the Old Covenant. Those who do this assume there is a distinction in Scripture (especially within Paul's letters) between the law as the revelation of God's abiding will on one hand, and legalism—the law misused by man to establish his own merit on the other. The context must dictate whether the text is referring to legitimate law or legalism. For example, "the works of the law" were perhaps in Paul's mind restricted to the signs of identification with the covenant— circumcision, Sabbath keeping, and ceremonial cleansing. This interpretation reflects an unhistorical approach, which fails to fully appreciate the unfolding drama of the Biblical story. In this view the New Covenant is seen as an "upgraded" version of the Old. Many who take this approach have also suggested there is a distinction between the moral Law of Moses (which abides today) and the ceremonial Law of Moses (which was terminated in Christ). They refer to passages like Matthew 23:23 and 1 Samuel 15:22. Most scholars recognize that a distinction between moral and ceremonial law is not clear in the Mosaic covenant. This is part of the problem in trying to mix the Old and New covenants. There is continuity between the Old Covenant and the New that must be expressed in ways that respect the important discontinuity that seems to be at the heart of Paul's teaching. This leads us to a third option.

Many students of Scripture see a discontinuity between the Old Covenant and New. This view contrasts the law (especially of Moses), and the grace of Christ as in Romans 6:14–15, 10:4, 2 Corinthians 3:3,6–18, Philippians 3:7–9. In this view an emphasis is placed on the New Testament epistles as the lens through which we read the Gospels and the Old Testament. The position expressed in this book tends to draw attention to the discontinuity between the Old and New Covenants. It sees a radical change with the coming of the New Covenant at the cross, resurrection, and Pentecost.

I maintain that the grace of God in Christ cannot be fully appreciated apart from a proper understanding of this discontinuity between the Old and New Covenants. It is the grace expressed through "the righteousness of faith" that liberates the soul and the whole life to a measure of freedom and joy that can only be described as revolutionary. This breastplate of armor (Eph.6:14) protects us, on the one hand, from pride of personal merit, and on the other, from despair of moral condemnation. Before this armor can be securely put in place however, we must face some perplexing questions raised from the Scripture itself. Satan loves to draw our attention to those texts of Scripture that seem to undermine the force of the imputed righteousness of Christ. The effect is one of creating serious doubts about the nature of our position in Christ or at least a good bit of confusion about God's grace. How are these troubling passages to be understood? In this appendix we will examine a number of the texts that raise questions in our minds about the truthfulness of God's radical grace.

If we work under the assumption the Scriptures are internally consistent—that is, they do not teach contradictory or mutually exclusive doctrines—then we need to seek harmony in our understanding of texts. Any such harmonization requires cautious, humble, and often tedious work. Note Satan's attack upon Christ in Matthew 4:1–11, where he used Scripture in a casual way that on the surface, seemed to make his point. After Christ's critique in response however, the force of Satan's argument evaporates. We too must compare Scripture with Scripture and seek to answer apparent contradictions in the texts of the Bible.

A problem passage is one that seems to contradict an accepted truth. A theme like "faith righteousness," when accepted as true, will leave a number of texts in need of clarification. Those who understand righteousness in terms of human performance will face a different set of problem passages. Each doctrinal position however will demand that careful attention be given to its unique problem passages. No matter what our convictions on this issue, we will have to address problem passages; and it is not always apparent how these passages are to be interpreted. One's theological assumptions will influence interpretation especially when the historical, literary, and grammatical contexts are inconclusive, which is sometimes the case.

It is my observation that many of the passages that are troublesome to the doctrines of "faith and righteousness" are troublesome for any concept of grace salvation, and therefore are difficult for every school of orthodox Protestantism. It seems that those who reject the teaching of "faith righteousness" on the basis of one or any number of the below-mentioned problem passages often would be unwilling to live with the logical conclusions of their own exegesis. Most of the passages under consideration seem to demand faithfulness, more than faith, with respect to justification before God. *"Without sanctification no man will see God"* (Heb.12:14) does not call for a partial or sincere effort at righteousness, but rather demands a perfect righteousness. No one but Christ could see God, for only He could meet such a standard.

My views do not necessarily represent the only possible or even the final word on each passage. I find myself unsure of how to understand some of these texts. That is why I see them as problem texts. My intention is twofold. First, I want to follow a straightforward reading of both the Old and New Testament in their respective covenantal contexts. Second, I want to offer an explanation that is plausible and in harmony with the doctrine of "faith righteousness," which I believe is so well established that it cannot be denied without a serious impeachment of orthodox Christianity. I am concentrating upon the New Testament material because of its more direct relevance to the meaning of the New Covenant of grace in Christ. The Old Testament material, for the most part, is best interpreted in the context of the Old Covenant of law. It goes without saying that my treatment will not be as detailed or exhaustive on each text as it could be.

No matter how heated the debate may be over this issue of righteousness, we must strive to work together as a body of sincere disciples in our struggle for true understanding of God and His kingdom. Many sincere and godly followers of Christ have strong feelings on differing sides of this issue. Let us all try to listen patiently, sympathetically, and critically with a motivation to grow in our knowledge of Christ and not just defend "our position." We must realize that much of what we see "dimly" in this life will be made clear only at Christ's coming. Let us not only be truth seekers but also Christ seekers and peacemakers. We will start our discussion with one of the

most familiar and challenging passages in the Gospels—
The Sermon on the Mount.

Matthew 5–7
"The Sermon on the Mount"

Reading these chapters brings a strong sense of awe at the
penetrating righteousness they demand. Furthermore the
righteousness called for is not to be outside the reader's
experience. Jesus calls for practical, experiential holiness—
the kind of holiness demanded by the law (5:17,20). The
last verse in chapter 5 summarizes this sermon: *"Therefore
you are to be perfect, as your heavenly Father is perfect."*
Entrance into heaven and security in one's relationship with
God are at stake as we read verses 21–23 of chapter 7: *"Not
everyone who says to me, 'Lord, Lord,' will enter the
kingdom of heaven, but only he who does the will of my
Father who is in heaven. Many will say to me on that day,
'Lord, Lord, did we not prophesy in your name, and in your
name drive out demons and perform many miracles?' Then
I will tell them plainly, 'I never knew you. Away from me,
you evildoers.'"*

     How can such teaching be harmonized with the
righteousness of faith?

1. This sermon reflects the orthodox teaching of the
   covenant that God made with Moses – a covenant of
   law, not grace (Jn.1:17 *"For the Law was given
   through Moses; grace and truth were realized
   through Jesus Christ"*). We will look in vain for
   Paul's doctrine of grace in the Sermon on the Mount.
   The teaching in these chapters is clearly conditional
   in nature. *"Whoever shall say, 'You fool,' shall be
   guilty enough to go into the hell of fire."* (5:22). *"But
   if you do not forgive men, then your Father will not
   forgive your transgressions"* (6:15). *"Every tree that
   does not bear good fruit is cut down and thrown into
   the fire"* (7:19).

2. When we understand Paul's explanation of the role of the law as a tutor (Gal.3:23–26) preparing us to appreciate Christ's work, we begin to see what Jesus is doing before His Jewish audience. Jesus is expounding the heart of the Mosaic Covenant (the law) in such a way that it puts everyone at a moral deficit. The Pharisees of Jesus' day had tamed the law so its "demands" could be met in the flesh. The Pharisee had postured himself to look good and feel good before the law and thus had become hard hearted and without ears to hear the coming message of the Messiah's Passion and substitutionary sacrifice. Jesus reinstated the cutting edge of the law so it would leave everyone hungering and thirsting for righteousness, having been "shut up under sin." *"For I say to you, that unless your righteousness surpasses that of the scribes and Pharisees, you shall not enter the kingdom of heaven"* (5:20). Although the ethical teachings in this sermon are valid and applicable to the church today, their intent is to bring all of us to our knees in despair. For not one of us has ever met the demands of the law, as expressed by Christ.

3. In Matthew 5:17–18, when Jesus says, *"Do not think that I have come to abolish the Law or the Prophets; I have not come to abolish them but to fulfill them. I tell you the truth, until heaven and earth disappear, not the smallest letter, not the least stroke of a pen, will by any means disappear from the Law until everything is accomplished,"* he is not suggesting that we will eventually meet the demands of the law, but rather that *he* will meet those demands. *He* will complete the law; *he* will accomplish all—even to the smallest stroke—so that at his death he could say, *"It is finished."* This is why Paul could say the Old Covenant (of law) was abolished or completed with Christ's death (Eph.2:15–16). He satisfied its demands completely. For any one of us to abolish the

demands of the law (before they are satisfied) and put them aside as irrelevant would be to undermine the atoning work of Christ on the cross to be a *"foolish builder"* (Matt.7:24-27) who does not take Jesus' words seriously.

4. To read this sermon outside its historical and theological context brings with it seemingly insurmountable obstacles in practical application. The conspicuous absence of grace and faith righteousness in this sermon should cause us to beware. I believe many of the "difficult" passages in Matthew, Mark, Luke, and John is best understood when seen in a pre-cross and pre-New Covenant light. While this sermon is written *for* our edification, it may not be written directly *about* us or *to* us. It must be seen through the lens of the New Covenant relationship that is explained so well in the writings of the Apostle Paul.

So how are Christians to use the Sermon on the Mount? First, we must recognize that this teaching is an exposition of the very nature of God's Spirit within His people. As we yield our lives to the control of the Spirit, we will be motivated to obey the high calling of Jesus in this sermon. Will we do so perfectly? Probably not! The Spirit wars against the flesh and the flesh against the Spirit so we do not always do what we please (Gal.5:17). Second, we must expect the Sermon on the Mount to have the same affect the law was to have. When we audit our lives carefully before its high demands, we should be convicted along with all others who are seeking security through personal moral discipline.

Matthew 7:15–23
"He who does the will of My Father"

In verses 21–23, Jesus seems to suggest our acceptance before God is based not upon our confession of faith but our obedience to the law. *"Not every one who says to Me,*

'Lord, Lord,' will enter the kingdom of heaven, but only he who does the will of my Father who is in heaven" (vs. 21).

Jesus' concern in this context is to distinguish between true and false prophets in Israel (vs. 15). His argument is centered upon the nature of their fruits. Those who speak for God are also going to follow after God. A person who fashioned himself a prophet of God, but was living independently of God's covenant requirements, was not to be recognized as a true prophet. Furthermore anyone who claimed to be of God and then ignored God's covenant law (practiced lawlessness) had no reason to feel secure. In applying this teaching to ourselves today, we must ask— What is God's covenant with us in Christ? The answer is seen in three texts—Romans 8:1–2, Hebrews 7:12, and 1 Corinthians 9:21. Anyone who confesses Christ and yet does not accept or abide within the covenant of grace through His blood is not to be received as a true child of God. We are expected to live exemplary moral lives in response to God's grace, but the central issue in New Covenant orthodoxy is faith not moral perfection.

Matthew 12:22–37
"The tree is known by its fruit"

In verse 33 Jesus seems to suggest we will be justified or condemned not on the basis of our faith in Christ but rather on the basis of our works. In this passage the issue is – recognizing and confessing Christ as the Son of God. The fruit (confession and direction) of a person's life reveals the nature of their spiritual identity. By rejecting God's Spirit and refusing to see Him in God's Son, the false prophets stand outside the covenant community. Recognition and confession are closely associated as are faith and baptism (see Matt.10:32–33; 12:36–37; Lk.12:8–10; Rom.10:1–11a). The point of this passage is not that our confession in general will be the measure of our salvation, but rather that our confession of Christ as God will be the fruit of true faith. If the "fruit" in this passage refers to the moral conduct of a person's life, we must ask, how ethically pure must a person be to be identified as a good tree? Was Peter who temporarily denied Christ a good tree? Was Paul, the chief of sinners, a good tree?

Matthew 18:7-11 (Mark 9:43-50)
"If your eye causes you to stumble, pluck it out"

Jesus' words here teach that if we "stumble" we will not inherit eternal life therefore whatever causes us to stumble must be removed to save our souls even to the point of physical dismemberment. But what does "stumble" mean in this passage? The same language is used in the parable of the soils to refer to those who "fall away" from the faith (Mark 4:17). This would suggest that we could understand "stumbling" as something more than backsliding into some menial sin. It probably refers to losing faith altogether. In other words it is better to be dismembered in this life than to lose the faith that leads to eternal life. The context in Mark's gospel is addressing our influence on those who are weaker in faith. The argument seems to be that when we "stumble" or fall away from faith we may cause others to fall away as well. One of the ways in which we do not cause our brothers to stumble is to remain strong in our own faith.

Matthew 18:21–35
"So shall My heavenly Father also do to you"

In Jesus' story of the unmerciful slave, He suggests that our faithfulness in forgiving others is a condition upon which our own forgiveness before God is based (see also Matt.6:14). If this is so, how are we to understand its relationship to the righteousness of faith?

As we seek to understand the significance of this story, we immediately recognize two difficulties (in addition to the apparent inconsistency mentioned above). First, there is the apparent difference between the extreme forbearance called forth from the disciples (vs. 21–22) and the lack of forbearance demonstrated by the King (God?) (vs. 32–35). Is Jesus actually suggesting we be more forgiving than God? Such an interpretation must certainly be reassessed. The second difficulty comes as we try to draw a parallel between the extracting of payment through torture (vs. 34) and our paying God in some way for our debt of sin to Him (vs. 35). It most certainly is not true that we can pay God off for our offenses. What then are the connection and more generally the meaning of this whole story?

Jesus wants to make one powerful point. In light of the greatness of God's forgiveness, we should be more than willing to forgive one another. The problem comes with verses 34–35. Because this teaching fits historically in the context of the Old Covenant (before Pentecost), it might be viewed as an example of law in action (as opposed to observing the contrast with grace—Eph.4:32); but I sense another explanation is needed. It is obvious to me that the story is not intended to provide a detailed parallel with our experience but rather to make a more general point. The torturers who await the unforgiving slave need to be understood *not* as instruments of God's condemnation of the unmerciful believer but rather as the natural consequences of his life choices. What goes around comes around. The way we treat others is the way we will be treated by others. It is interesting to note that the verb form of the Greek word translated *"torturers"* is used to describe illness—Matthew 4:24, 8:6, or spiritual anguish of life (resulting from bitterness). In other words if we who are forgiven refuse to forgive, we can expect not only to be treated the same way by others but also to suffer the natural consequence of bitterness. Empathy is so important that God will go to great lengths to teach it to us. We can learn it the easy way (being treated graciously) or the hard way (being treated justly). The second book in this series *"Peace Makers"* addresses this passage more fully.

Matthew 19:16–29, Mark 10:17-30, Luke 18:18-30
"The rich young ruler"

In this passage Jesus responds to the question: "What shall I do to inherit eternal life?" He answers by saying "you know the commandments" (vs.20) suggesting that holiness is the key to eternal life. This is consistent with the Old Covenant's message where commitment to "do the works of the law" (be holy) was expected of those who would be identified with the community of God. In the Sermon on the Mount Jesus suggests that a person under the law is to hunger and thirst for a righteousness that they did not have, and according to Paul, could not achieve in and of themselves (Matt.5:6). Jesus focuses attention on the source of the young man's hope, "give up that which is the source of your security in this life (your material wealth) and follow me." This might be expressed as, "Repent—turn from the present source of your hope to follow me, the new source of your hope." A key to understanding this passage is in vs.30 where Jesus says that those who transfer their hope from the things of this life to hope in him will not be disappointed in that what they receive will be greater than what they leave.

Matthew 24:50-51 (Luke 12:46)
"Assigned a place with the unbelievers."

In a passage that addresses the conduct of those who are not alert or prepared for the Lord's appearance there will be dire consequences. Luke tells us that they will be *"assigned a place with unbelievers."* Matthew tells us they will be *"cut in pieces and assigned a place with the hypocrites; in that place there will be weeping and gnashing of teeth."* In the context of the Old Covenant Jesus may be saying that true believers in Israel (the remnant) are those who long for and look for the true Messiah while others do not.

Matthew 25:31–46
"The sheep and the goats"

In this passage Jesus is describing the nature of the final judgment of the Gentiles (nations). Again the emphasis is on how they behaved toward *"his people."* Those who were merciful, kind, and showed love to the Son of man through His people would be rewarded with eternal life; and those who were delinquent would receive eternal punishment.

At face value this text seems to contradict the whole gospel message of grace so well established in Paul's Epistles. Indeed it completely destroys any "good news" in the Gospel, for it implies that only those who love will be loved and only those who save others will be saved from eternal punishment themselves. Many interpreters suggest that the judgment described is the general final judgment, and the criteria is the fruit of faith, not just the merit of the person apart from active trust in God. Some suggest that the judgment refers only to Gentile nations during "the great tribulation" and has to do with their treatment of Israel determining whether or not they enter the millennial kingdom.

There is another way of looking at this text that I believe makes more sense and avoids the dilemma of justification by works. The references to feeding, welcoming, clothing, and visiting can be understood as representative acts of sharing in the community of God's family where others are accepted as kin (in the Spirit). The point of the passage seems to be that the reception of Christ and His Church cannot be separated. To receive Christ means we must also receive His people, His Body, His Church. If we can't receive His people, we probably haven't received Him. The focus of attention is not upon what is done but rather to whom it is done. The nature of the judgment then is centered upon the reception or rejection of Christ and His Body, the Church. This truth is repeated elsewhere in Jesus' and Paul's teaching (see

Matt.10:40–42; 18:3–6; Lk.10:16; Jn.13:20; Gal.4:14). We might note that "*brothers*" (vs.40) is never used to describe the human race. It refers either to the covenant family of faith or to ethnic kin.

John 5:28–29
"Good deeds and life"

How can the doctrine of justification by faith be reconciled with this text, which links the resurrection of life with good deeds? The options seem to be as follows:

1. The believers (like the non-believers) will face eternal life or condemnation based upon their deeds in this life. The believers will, by the power of the Holy Spirit, be expected to live righteous lives and thus inherit the blessing. The problems with this interpretation are numerous:

    a. How righteous does a person have to be in their deeds before they are counted worthy of life?

    b. How many Christians are righteous enough (even with the help of the Holy Spirit) to be confident of eternal life?

    c. Would it not be fair to assume that some non-believers would have better or at least as good deeds as some believers?

    d. How can a "gospel" be good news with this seemingly impossible challenge looming before the believer?

    e. How does this interpretation differ from the legal system where a person's performance was emphasized over the righteousness of faith?

    f. How does this view differ from the doctrine of the Pharisees of Jesus' day? Did they not believe it was God's enabling grace that gave them power to obey?

2. The believer's faith will be evident in his deeds so that at the resurrection and judgment the good deeds will reflect

175

faith. In other words, we have here a faith validated by works. I have questions about this view as well:

a. If faith is the issue, why doesn't Jesus mention it as the issue?

b. It seems to me that as soon as we insist that experiential holiness be a signal of positional holiness, we are right back under law. The only addition is a new power source to help us be more successful in keeping the law.

3. This is an unsolvable enigma we cannot understand until the revelation of Christ. If this is the case, then where am I to find any security and peace in this life? Should I not do everything I can to try to live a perfect life with the outside chances Jesus will at least reward my efforts? Is this good news? Not to most of us.

4. There is another way of understanding these views that may be preferable to the above options. Note what Jesus said earlier in this context (vs. 24)—"*I tell you the truth, whoever hears my word and believes him who sent me has eternal life and will not be condemned; he has crossed over from death to life.*" This verse seems to clearly say that faith in God automatically grants eternal life. There is no hint that faith leads to good deeds that in turn qualify a person for life. This emphasis is seen in other parts of John's writings— 1:12–13; 3:18; 20:31; 1 John 5:13. John later says in chapter 6:28–29—"*Then they asked him, 'What must we do to do the works God requires?' Jesus answered, 'The work of God is this: to believe in the one he has sent.'*" (See 1 Jn.3:23). In John's gospel, "doing the good" and "committing the evil" (5:29) may be a direct (not an indirect) reference to faith in Christ. He may be talking specifically about faith (as deeds) in these verses, but not about deeds that issue from faith.

John 15:1–6
"The fruitful branches"

In this portion of Jesus' teachings we are led to believe that the status of a believer (branch) with respect to Christ (the vine) is dependent upon the believer's *"fruitfulness"* (vs. 2,5–6), not his position or faith. The key to this passage rests with our understanding of the meaning of *"in Me"* (vs. 2). Does Jesus use this phrase to designate a person who is *"in Christ"* in the same way Paul uses it in his Epistles (Eph.1)? If so, then we must conclude John 15 is speaking of two kinds of Christians—fruitful and secure, alongside the unfruitful and insecure. If however Jesus uses this phrase in a more general way to describe His twelve disciples (including Judas), we have a different context. In this context Jesus may be explaining to His disciples the significance of what will happen to Judas Iscariot, the one who proves to be fruitless and is cast away. We must note that even though Judas was chosen as a disciple and therefore a "branch in Me," he was not truly *"of us"* or *"in Christ"* in the Pauline sense of that phrase (see Jn.6:64,71). The fruitfulness consists of all that issues forth from abiding in Christ. Those who have such a relationship are disciplined (*"pruned,"* vs. 2) while those who do not have such a relationship will be excluded (*"burned,"* vs. 6). We must resist the temptation to read into this passage, Paul's teaching of union with Christ through the baptism with the Spirit. Jesus' words in John fifteen came before the Spirit was given (Jn.7:39, Acts 4:33).

Acts 3:26
"Turn from their wicked ways"

The blessing of Christ will come only as the people "turn from their wicked ways." What does this mean? There are two ways of looking at verse 26. 1) The blessings come only as we bring our lives under successful management so that we no longer sin in any way. Those who hold this view usually modify it to refer to "intentional sins." This view creates some difficult scenarios. For example, it suggests we are not saved by grace but by empowerment to keep the law. 2) The "wicked ways" in question are the sins mentioned in verses 13–15. The sins in view here are 1) refusing to identify with Christ as "our Savior" and 2) participating in His execution. This is the preferred interpretation in my view. If Christ has taken away our sins, then the issue standing between God and us is Christ, not our lack of moral power to keep the law.

Acts 5:1–11
"Ananias and Sapphira"

This passage is troubling in that the offense of Ananias and Sapphira (to lie to the Spirit) seems to be met with instant and severe judgment (they fall dead). The grace shown Peter and even Judas by Jesus along with the message of forgiveness preached by Peter would suggest that at least an opportunity to repent was in order. The nearly universal assumption among commentators is that the deaths are the result of God's judgment. But is this really clear? Nowhere is the reason for or source of the deaths explained. The text indicates that those who heard of this were afraid, but it does not indicate they were afraid of God. Is it possible that the social shame or some other personal response is the cause of the death? The text simply does not give us the details. Every card that sin deals says "death" on it. To play in the card game of sin is to invite one's own death. The more one sins, the closer his or her death approaches (and the more miserable his or her present experience becomes). Being eternally secure does not exempt believers from the death-dealing consequences of sin. It is possible to read this text as a dramatic and uncommon form of God's discipline. It is obvious that not every instance of this kind of offense was met with the same experience.

Acts 5:32
"Those who obey"

Peter's words here suggest that the reception of the Holy Spirit (the mark of every Christian) is dependent upon the person's obedience. We must ask the question "What kind of obedience?" Note the following texts: Acts 6:7 *"obedient to the faith,"* John 3:36 where *"believing"* is parallel to *"obey,"* John 6:29 *"this is the work of God, that you believe in Him whom He has sent."* It is not obedience to the law that Peter is concerned about here, but rather the obedience of faith. Note Galatians 3:2: *"This is the only thing I want to find out from you: did you receive the Spirit by the works of the law, or by hearing with faith?"*

Romans 2:1–16
"Rendering to every man according to his deeds"

In these verses Paul clearly suggests that the basis of our acceptance by God is our *"deeds"* (vs. 6–10). It is not the *"hearer of the law"* that is just before God, but the *"doer of the Law"* (vs. 13). In order to appreciate Paul's argument, we must look at the broader context of his letter to the Romans. In verses 16 and 17 of chapter one he reveals the thesis of his letter, which centers upon the righteousness of faith. In order to develop his thesis, he first must demonstrate the need on the part of all mankind for faith righteousness. He does this in chapters 1–3 by showing how everyone (Jew or Gentile) is guilty before a God who evaluates people on the basis of their performance and motives. The point of 2:1–16 is summarized in chapter 3:9–20—*"both Jews and Greeks are all under sin" and "through the Law comes the knowledge of sin."* Some of the Jews took pride in their discernment of God's will (they were hearers of the law), but this did not bring them closer to God. God does not justify man on the basis of what he knows (his keen discernment of right and wrong), but rather on what he does. A person could conceivably (in the minds of some of his readers) be justified before God by living a perfect life (keeping the Law of Moses or faithfully following their conscience), but no one has or will ever be able to do that perfectly. This is why there is a need for redemption and substitution. The righteousness *of faith* is vital to life. Chapter 2:1–16 is a tongue-in-cheek invitation to stand before a holy God and see how we look. The results will prepare us to listen to Paul's thesis—all need the righteousness of faith. In summary this text is presenting a hypothetical picture of what man can expect in facing a holy God without the hope of the gospel. Without the righteousness of faith we are clothed only in our own righteousness and will stand or fall on the basis of our deeds.

Romans 4:10
"The judgment seat of God"

This text and the following texts—2 Corinthians 5:10; 1 Corinthians 3:11–15; 4:5—refer to the "Bema" or judgment seat of God (or Christ). These passages refer to a special judgment of true believers—not to determine their spiritual life or death, but rather to assign their rewards (praise or crowns) or lack of rewards in heaven. It is a judgment of "disclosure," not "damnation." It is the place where believers will see in their fruitfulness the hand of God's Spirit and in their folly the covering of God's grace. 1 Corinthians 3:11–15 is the most helpful text to outline the nature of this special judgment. Note that verse 15 suggests it is possible to fare poorly in this judgment and yet not forfeit eternal life - "*If any man's work is burned up, he will suffer loss; but he himself will be saved, yet so as through fire.*" (1 Cor.3:15). The nature of the judgment centers on the quality of one's ministry. Was the ministry built with and upon the eternal and imperishable Word of God or upon something else? In short, this judgment has nothing to do with eternal life. It is to *disclose* the true nature, source, and result of our inner motives and outer deeds.

Romans 6:22
"Resulting in sanctification,
and the outcome, eternal life."

Justification by faith frees us from sin and death while it enslaves us to God. This results in "sanctification", which brings with it eternal life. "Sanctification" here is not to be understood as "active righteousness" or "practical holiness" but rather as the setting aside "in Christ" as in 1 Corinthians 1:2 where Paul recognizes the Corinthians as sanctified even though they were yet sinners in practice. Eternal life is the outcome of being declared righteous (holy) by faith.

Romans 8:4
"The requirements of the law fulfilled in us"

To many readers these texts suggests that although one cannot expect to be holy (perfectly obey the law of God) in the power of the flesh, once the Spirit has come such holiness is expected as one lives in the power of the Spirit. Again the obligation to live a sinless life is implied for all who are indwelt by God's Spirit. For most of God's people this is not so easy or comforting since they find themselves more familiar with the experience described in Romans 7:14–25 (even after knowing the Spirit's presence) than the experience implied in Romans 8:4.

The key to understanding this text is found in the broader context of Romans 7–8. Paul's argument seems to develop as follows: As long as I am in this human "fallen" state "under the law", I will be unable to live a life of obedience perfectly satisfying the demands of God's holy law. Because I can aspire to perfection in my mind but not attain to it in my body, I experience dissonance. I am miserable, restless, anxious, and condemned (Rom.7:14–25). This is exactly what the "law of God" was designed to do—show me my hopeless, helpless, fallen state and leave me so miserable I would long for and respond to the message of God's grace in Christ (see Gal.3:24; Rom.3:19–20). I am "let off the hook" by being "set free" from the obligation to keep the law of God for salvation when I am "in Christ." I am now under a New Covenant based on Christ's perfect performance *for* me, not his work *through* me (Rom.8:1–3, 7:1–13). Romans 8:5–15 seems to be saying we must set our minds within the context of the

New Covenant and not the Old if we are to have life and peace before God. If we are "in the flesh," that is, seeing ourselves in the context of the Old Covenant (delinquent before the law of God in our human frailty); we die or stand condemned, having no peace of mind. Walking according to the flesh or the Spirit is (in this context) not our actual performance so much as a "mindset" or perspective on our view of self apart from Christ or "in Christ."

Now we come again to verse 4, which I find to be a difficult text. It could be understood to suggest that the Spirit empowers the believer to fulfill all the demands of the law, or it could mean that the laws demands are fulfilled in Christ. This latter view sees the requirements of the law fulfilled not "by us" but "in us" through the New Covenant principle of "Christ in us the hope of Glory"—Christ having lived the perfect life for us. This is the mindset of peace. Faith becomes a source of peace in our lives as we set our mind on the Christ of the New Covenant, not the flesh. The passive verb "be fulfilled" supports the idea that it is not "our doing" that is in view here. The preceding verses (vs.1–3) are focused upon the substitutionary work of Christ further suggesting it is Christ's work "for us" that is in view in verse 4.

We also must note that vs.4 indicates that the demands of the law will be *fulfilled* (fully met) by those who are in the Spirit. The only way in which the demands of the law are *fully* met is through the imputed perfect righteousness of Christ. It is quite evident that these demands are not fully met by followers of Christ who are imperfect in their obedience. It has been correctly observed that the essence of the fulfillment of the law is the believer's "love for one another" (Rom.13:8–10, Gal.5:13–15, Matt.7:12, 22:37–40), and in this sense we can and should expect to see believers as salt and light in the world—fulfilling the law. But it still must be observed that no one loves perfectly all the time.

It also must be noted. *". . . you are not in the flesh but in the Spirit, if indeed the Spirit of God dwells in you. But if anyone does not have the Spirit of Christ, he does not belong to Him."* (vs.9) This would suggest that all who *"belong to Christ"* *"have the Spirit of Christ"* are *"in the Spirit"*, *"have their mind set on the Spirit"*, and *"walk according to the Spirit."* Are all who *"belong to Christ"* perfect? Yes, but only if they see their righteousness as the righteousness of faith in Christ. Look at Galatians 5:16-26 as a parallel to Romans 7:14-8:17.

Romans 8:13
"Living according to the flesh, ... you must die"
"Putting to death the deeds of the body ... shall live"

This verse is a summary of Romans chapter 6 where we are taught the only way to escape Adam is through death—either: 1) our death in the judgment or 2) our union with Christ's death in baptism. To live according to the flesh for a Christian does not mean the potential loss of eternal life (heaven), but rather the need to reaffirm the truths of water baptism as expressed in Romans 6.

The second part of the verse sounds as though eternal life is only possible for those who have conquered the deeds of the body. If this is true, then the argument of Romans 1–7 is meaningless. What Paul has in view here is "life in the Spirit," which cannot be experienced unless the deeds of the body are being put to death. If we are to experience "spiritual vitality" in this present life, we must cooperate with the leading of the Spirit and not the flesh. Part of taking our water baptism seriously involves saying "NO!" to the flesh. This is a discipline and process that is a part of our spiritual maturation in this life.

1 Corinthians 5:5
"That his spirit may be saved"

The salvation of the spirit in the day of the Lord Jesus is a parallel to 1:8, *"who shall also confirm you to the end, blameless in the day of our Lord Jesus Christ."* The *"blameless"* here was probably a reference to the confirmation of the Corinthian's faith. Their conduct certainly was not blameless. The phrase *"that his spirit may be saved in the day of the Lord Jesus"* suggests the person in question who is a *"so called brother"* (vs. 11) might be an unregenerate hypocrite in need of saving faith which, given his conduct, he appears not to have. A Christian who acts this way is expected to have shame.

This would suggest to us that the purpose of the disciplining of the immoral person in 1 Corinthians 6:5 was to bring him to true faith. In Matthew 18:17 we are told that a brother who does not respond to discipline should (in extreme cases) be treated as a non-believer.

1 Corinthians 6:9–11
"Unrighteous will not inherit the kingdom"

This text suggests that people who are unrighteous (fornicators, idolaters, adulterers, effeminate, homosexuals, thieves, covetous, drunkards, revilers, swindlers) will not go to heaven. Paul indicates some of the Corinthians *"were"* like this but not anymore. The immediate context (vs.1–8) talks about the "unrighteous" judges in the world who are outside the faith. This is the *"unrighteous"* Paul has in mind as a point of reference. He is not suggesting the Corinthians were perfectly free (in their walk) of all the sins mentioned. What Paul does understand is that "in Christ" Christians are free from the law and the condemnation it associates with sin, because His righteousness is imputed to them. He has already established the fact that the Corinthians were *"saints in Christ"* (1:2) but were living as sinners (3:1–3). Those outside of Christ live in a state of condemnation because of their sin. Believers escape that judgment because Christ was judged for them (Rom.7:21–8:3). The implication is— strive to live up to your new life in Christ, and do so not to gain eternal life, but because this is the new nature that Christ has given you. Those outside the faith (who stand only on their own moral record) are condemned for these deeds. Don't mock your freedom in Christ by foolishly doing what they do. Note other references to the believer as a new person in Christ— 2 Corinthians 5:16–17, Ephesians 2:1–10.

1 Corinthians 9:27
"Disqualified"

In 1 Corinthians 9:27 Paul expresses his fear of being disqualified if he does not bring his body into subjection. The important question is from what would he be disqualified—eternal life, rewards for faithful service, integrity, or ministry? The answer is found in the context of the passage (both before and after). In Chapter 9:19–23 he is concerned with the laying aside of his personal taste and culture for the sake of those to whom he is ministering. He must be selfless and become all things to all men (vs. 22). He sees this sacrifice as a legitimate part of "partaking" in the gospel. He is to illustrate the truth of grace as well as proclaim it. In Chapter 9:24–26 he speaks of his life as a race being run with a goal, and for a prize. The goal is the "winning" or "saving" of some (vs. 22). He disciplines himself (vs. 27) so he will not be a hypocrite but a true example of what he preaches. The Greek word translated *"disqualified"* has the idea of "disapproved" or "illegitimate." Paul is concerned not about losing his eternal life but about losing his authenticity as Christ's ambassador.

1 Corinthians 10:1–21
"Perish"

The children of Israel who were redeemed by blood from bondage in Egypt were tempted and fell into idolatry. They switched religions and worshiped a golden calf (Ex.32:1–10). They committed immorality (marrying foreign women and their gods) (Num.25:1–2). In chapter eight Paul had warned those who were strong in faith to be careful lest they cause those weak in faith to be mislead and *"perish"* or *"be ruined"* (1 Cor.8:11). This is the same term used in

John 3:16 and 1 Corinthians 1:18 where it is linked to exclusion from eternal life.

Paul is not suggesting the Corinthians can lose their salvation by failing to live a sinless life, but he is suggesting if they turn from faith in Christ, they will not have any *claim* on eternal life. It was possible for a weak believer to be misled and return to the pagan temple gods in Corinth.

Our security is not tied to our moral conduct, but it is tied to our faith confession. Israel's failure was its turning from YHWH to the golden calf, which was pictured in its craving evil, immoral worship, trying God, grumbling, etc. We are secure in Christ by faith. If there is no faith, there is no security. Our security is not conditioned upon our works but upon our connection to the Cross of Christ by faith.

1 Corinthians 11:32
"Judged along with the world"

The Corinthian Christians were exhorted to judge themselves lest they be disciplined by God so as to not be *"condemned along with the world."* This suggests that a believer could lose salvation grace as a result of not responding to discipline and correcting sinful conduct. When we look at a parallel context in 1 Corinthians 5:8 where the *"cleaning out of the old leaven"* is a part of proper observance of the Lord's table, we get some idea of what kind of behavior is in view. The judgment of God in 1 Corinthians 5:5 suggests that the body (flesh) may be disciplined lest the soul be lost. In other words a person's physical life will be affected before apostasy would take place. The reference in 1 Corinthians 11:30 to "sick, weak, and sleep (death)" seems to parallel 1 Corinthians 5:5.

1 Corinthians 15:2
"Unless you believed in vain"

This passage suggests one could have faith (really believe) and yet not derive any benefit from faith because it lacked something—good works perhaps. The context of Paul's argument in chapter fifteen is that one could not deny the resurrection and still have a rational hope for eternal life. Faith was no better than its object. In this case the object was the resurrected Christ (vs.14,17). It was not "good works" that would keep faith from being vain but the dead body of Jesus. If Christ was not raised, there is no hope of eternal life no matter how strongly a person might believe it. Our faith affects eternal hope because Christ was indeed raised from the dead not because we have been faithful in keeping the law of God.

Galatians 5:16–26
"I have forewarned you, that those who practice such things will not inherit the kingdom of God"

Galatians 5:21 suggests anyone who practices the "*deeds of the flesh*"—*immorality, impurity, sensuality, idolatry, sorcery, enmities, strife, jealousy, outbursts of anger, disputes, dissensions, factions, envying, drunkenness, carousing, etc.*—will not inherit the kingdom of God. 1 Cor.6:9; Eph.5:5; Col.3:6 make similar assertions. When we look at the context of this passage, we gain some insight into its meaning. In Galatians 5:24 Paul reminds us that all those who belong to Christ have crucified (died to) the flesh with its passions. In the next verse he invites those who "*live by the Spirit*" (justified by faith) to now also "*walk by the Spirit*" (serve one another in love). In verse 16 Paul tells his Christian readers when they *walk by the Spirit*, they will not "*carry out*" (carry out to the end) or "*practice*" (commit to) the works of the flesh, which are illustrated by examples in vs.19-21 and are not acts of love.

Some implications are clear. 1) It is possible to *live by the Spirit* and not consistently or perfectly *walk by the*

Spirit. If this were not possible, why would Paul be exhorting Christians to walk by the Spirit. 2) All who belong to Jesus have put to death the passions of the flesh in their baptism. But this does not mean they no longer experience fleshly passions, especially when they put themselves back under the law (vs.18). Romans 7:21–8:3, may be an explanation of Galatians 5:18. 3) All who are *in the flesh* do not live by the Spirit, being outside faith in Christ (Rom.8:8-9). They are committed to a world of selfish, carnal, attitudes and actions. This kind of life cannot please God and will face exclusion from the kingdom of God (Rom.8:5-8).   There are two ways by which a person can be seen as outside God's grace and outside Christ. First, they can find their hope in obedience to the law apart from faith in Christ. Second, they can give themselves over to the flesh with a thoroughly pagan mindset. See 1 Corinthians 6:9–11 above. Authentic faith cannot exist with either of these heresies. Those who are wholly committed to live by the flesh are not in Christ no matter what their superficial confession of faith might be. They will not inherit eternal life. True Christians may not be perfect, but they will live with tension between flesh and Spirit. They cannot and will not be wholly given over to the *practices* of the flesh. Paul says this knowing that if a person has the Spirit of Christ they will not live in the flesh, nonetheless he warns them to stay away from all behaviors, which exclude unbelievers from eternal life. ("entering the kingdom" is linked with eternal life in Matt.25:31-46, Mk.10:17-31, 1 Cor.15.)

Galatians 6:6–10
"Sowing and reaping"

Paul warns us that to sow to the flesh means corruption, while to sow to the Spirit will mean a harvest of eternal life (vs. 8). Is he suggesting the way we live our lives will determine our security before God? Look at the context of these verses. "*6 And let the one who is taught the word share all good things with him who teaches. 7 Do not be deceived, God is not mocked; for whatever a man sows, this he will also reap. 8 For the one who sows to his own flesh shall from the flesh reap corruption, but the one who sows to the Spirit shall from the Spirit reap eternal life."* He is addressing himself to the relationship between those who teach the Word and those who receive the teaching (vs. 6). In summary he is saying, "If the student is selfish and unwilling to share his resources with the teacher (sowing to the Spirit), then he will reap accordingly." This same idea of sowing money for God's work is contained in 2 Corinthians 9:6, *"Now this I say, he who sows sparingly shall also reap sparingly; and he who sows bountifully shall also reap bountifully."* The reference to *"eternal life"* in verse eight has to do with the blessings that come from sowing to the Spirit in the sense of supporting the proclamation of the Word. When a person supports the teaching of the Word of God and receives that instruction, they will reap a harvest of eternal life, which is the result of the Word's work in a person. The passage is not suggesting that if a person sins, they disqualify themselves from eternal life.

Philippians 1:6
"perfecting the work that he began"

Paul speaks of his confidence *"that He who began a good work in you will perfect it until the day of Christ Jesus."* The context (vs.3–7) relates not to personal salvation but to the participation of the Philippians with Paul in his ministry needs (4:10–20). We might also review 2 Corinthians 8–9 to get an idea of the relationship of giving to participate in the spread of the Gospel. The good work of giving to support Paul was expected to continue until the end.

Philippians 2:12
"Work out your salvation with fear and trembling ..."

These words suggest our salvation is conditioned upon our faithfulness in action and not upon faith alone. It appears more probable that Paul's concern here is not with our individual destiny so much as our corporate responsibility. Paul exhorts the Philippians in verses 1–11 to follow Christ's example of selfless humility by serving one another, thus displaying an outworking of their relationship to God. They are to be in awe (fear and trembling) of the simple fact that God is at work in their lives (vs.13). As a body of believers they are to live out their faith in their relationships with one another in awe of God's imminence.

Becoming a Christian and becoming a good disciple of Christ do not happen at the same time. It takes time and practice to become a mature, effective disciple. For this reason, God said, '*Work out your salvation*'. We do not work to obtain or keep our salvation, which is a free gift through faith. But we do need to see our salvation work its way into all areas of life. In this sense we are in the process of seeing our salvation produce the fruits of salvation in relationships through space and time, here and now. We usher the Spirit of Christ into our lives by faith. We usher that same Spirit out through our lives as we obey.

Colossians 3:5–6
"These things bring wrath"

This text and others like it (1 Cor.6:9; Eph.5:6; Gal.5:19-21; 2 Pet.3:11) argue that Christians (who are God's children) should not live like those who will experience God's wrath. There is not necessarily a direct link between the Christian who practices sin and the wrath of God in these texts. The inconsistency of being children of God and then living like God's enemies (who will be punished for their rebellion) is the point of these passages. An ambassador from another country is immune from prosecution in American courts for minor traffic violations. He or she should be reminded however that it is important to obey the traffic laws, which bring a fine to others who break them. The suffering of Christ for all who believe illustrates the seriousness of sin and the nature of the wrath it incurs.

1 Timothy 4:16
"As you do this you will insure salvation (save) both for yourselves and those who hear you"

"*As you do this*" is linked to the teaching of the Gospel, which involves abiding faith in Jesus Christ. It is orthodox teaching that ensures salvation when it is received by faith. The core of that teaching is the hope we have in Christ as our Savior, through faith (vs.10 "*we have fixed our hope on the living God, who is the Savior of all men, especially of believers.*"). This is what Timothy was to teach (vs.11 "*Prescribe and teach these things.*").

1 Timothy 5:8
"Worse than an unbeliever"

In this text we have a good example of how a failure to recognize the spirit of a passage can lead us to rather fantastic conclusions. Some might, for example, try to suggest that unless a person provides for his family financially; he is not only a non-believer (denying the faith) but actually worse off than those who have never believed. Isn't it much more likely that Paul is saying—"If we are Christians and yet don't carry out the natural responsibilities of life (caring for our families), we are behaving worse than the heathen and are refusing to accept the obvious implications of our faith." Sadly there are many genuine believers who have conducted themselves in specific areas of life or at certain times in such a way that others, who do not have a faith relationship with the living God, put them to shame. This is why Paul exhorts believers to walk in a manner worthy of their calling.

Hebrews 3:7–19
"Falling away from the living God"

In this passage we find a number of warnings that can be very unsettling for the one who is not living a life of perfect obedience and holiness (see vs. 10–12). If we are to correctly understand this passage, we must note that the clear Old Testament parallel of the Israelites in the wilderness is a model given to us as a warning (vs. 7–11,16–19). But how is our spiritual experience parallel to theirs? What is the meaning of *"rest"* for us? Is it heaven, the victorious life here on earth, or something else? Were those Israelites who left Egypt, but failed to enter Palestine, representing true believers with a weak faith or were they apostates?

Without taking the time to present a detailed exposition, let me offer an explanation that seems to fit the historical and literary contexts. The salvation of God has many aspects. It is something we have (complete) in Christ, and yet it is something we are growing into (Phil.2:12) and do not yet have in its completed form (1 Thess.5:9, 1 Pet.1:5). It can be compared to physical adoption into a new family. Even though the adoption may be legally complete, there is much to learn and "grow into" in order to live like a son or daughter with new privileges and responsibilities.

Part of our problem with Hebrews three stems from our tendency to view salvation only as a completed act and see everything subsequent to our initial commitment to Christ as relatively insignificant or secondary. The New Testament portrait however is more holistic and emphasizes the outworking of salvation as a vital extension of the initial response to Christ.

The best understanding of the spiritual state of the Israelites in the wilderness sees them as true believers (covered by Passover blood) who have not followed through in their faith to experience all God has for them. This rebellion brought God's discipline just as it did in 1 Corinthians 11:27–34 (see also Heb.12). In the same way we today can fall short of entering into all God has for us when we become hardened by sin, fall away from vibrant trust in God, and force Him to discipline us as a father would a wayward child. Heaven and hell are not the issues here. The passage is dealing with spiritual growth and retardation, feast and famine.

Hebrews 5:9
"All who obey"

This text links eternal salvation with obedience suggesting that works, not faith, is the real issue. The real question has to do with the meaning of obedience in this context. Is it obedience to every command of Christ, or is it the obedience of faith? If the former is correct, not one of us has eternal life. If the latter is correct, we have no contradiction with justification by faith. The text says nothing about partial obedience or trying to obey. This text supports "works salvation" or refers to the obedience, which is the act of faith (Jn.6:29 *"This is the work of God, that you believe in Him whom He has sent."*).

Hebrews 6:4–12
"Falling away"

The section from 5:11–6:2 is an exhortation to genuine Christians who are spiritually immature. It invites them to go beyond elementary gospel teaching and *"press on to maturity."* A Christian who thinks he or she needs to initiate salvation all over again every time they sin will never grow.

The *"foundation"* (6:1–2) is a description of the initiation to true Christian experience. We are speaking of genuine Christians (6:3–5) who sin *"falling away"* (6:6). The verb for *"fallen away"* has the meaning of "a misdeed or trespass" in its noun form. It is used by Paul in Galatians 5:4 of falling from grace back into or under law. Upon falling into a sin, these Christians may have mistakenly thought they had to go back to the starting line of the race and start all over again. Note how often the expression *"again"* is found—"not laying *again* a foundation" (6:1); "renew them *again* unto repentance, crucifying *again*" (6:6). A major theme of the next several chapters is the "once-for-all" nature of Christ's work and our initiation into a secure relationship with him—7:25–27; 9:11–12, 24–28; 10:1–4, 10–14. The point of the passage is that it is logically impossible to go through the initial steps of coming to Christ again every time we sin. Repentance in this passage is the initial strategic repentance of coming to faith in Christ (vs.1 *"repentance from dead works"*) not the tactical repeated repentance of daily life.

These Hebrew believers came out of an Old Covenant background where every time they sinned they had to bring a new sacrifice. It would now be insulting to the Cross of Christ with its "once for all" effect to repeat the sacrifice of Christ over and over again.

The term *"impossible"* in verse six creates a seemingly insurmountable obstacle to interpretations that see this text as referring to apostasy in that it precludes the possibility of a change of heart. If a person is free to turn away from faith in Christ are we to suggest they are not free to turn back to faith in him? This seems to defy all we know of the biblical portrayal of man and all we observe of man from our experience. It is far more likely that the *"impossible"* has to do with the logic of the issue, not the will of the person. If you reject grace and choose to go back and live under law there is no provision for forgiveness as the Old (law) Covenant has been terminated as a system of atonement and repentance.

The following verses (6:7–12) suggest no good can come from failing to make progress by constantly returning to renew our initiation into the kingdom of God. Hebrews 6 and 10 can be addressed together because, in my estimation, they refer to the same basic issue—we cannot and need not be reconverted every time we sin.

Hebrews 10:26–31
"Sinning willfully"

The Old Covenant prescribed repeated sacrifices for sins (as sins were committed). Some Jewish believers may have asked, "Do we need to retrace our steps in converting to faith in Christ, every time we sin?" The writer of Hebrews instructs his readers that with the New Covenant of grace in

Christ, the Old Covenant was terminated. The Old Covenant is no longer available as a means to handle guilt. *"There no longer remains a sacrifice for sins"* (vs. 26). If you go on willfully sinning and do not cling in faith to the finished work of the Christ of the New Covenant but try to make atonement via the relics of the Old Covenant's repeated sacrifices, you are living in a fantasy world (see vs. 29). The Old Covenant provision has been terminated and replaced by the New Covenant provision—faith in Christ who is a *"once for all time"* sacrifice for sins. Without that faith one is left to face the righteous judgment of God (vs. 29–31) with no hope. If those who set aside the Law of Moses were judged harshly, how much more vulnerable will one be who rejects the sacrifice for sin at the cross. Don't lose faith in the work of Christ on the cross. It is this loss of faith that is the sin of vs.26.

Hebrews 12:14
"Sanctification and seeing God"

This text is troublesome because it suggests the believers to whom it is addressed are to pursue holiness in order to *"see the Lord."* The "sanctification" mentioned here is often used to describe the "holiness" every true believer possesses by virtue of his or her sharing in Christ. In this sense it has nothing to do with our experiential faithfulness before the law but is rather a description of imputed righteousness. But in what way can this text have this sense when it exhorts believers to "pursue" sanctification as though it were something they did not yet possess?

First we must note if we wish to understand "sanctification" (used here) as experiential (not imputed) holiness, then we are to 1) declare that *"seeing the Lord"* is the result of our moral performance and not grace/faith, and 2) also conclude that no person will ever see God, for no one will ever achieve "experiential sanctification" in this life (see 1 Jn.1:8).

A perfectly natural interpretation avoiding the above problems would be the following:

1. *"Seeing the Lord"* depends on perfect sanctification, which is granted to us (positionally) through faith in Christ and experientially at glorification or the resurrection of the believer.

2. Since this is our ultimate destination (holiness, perfection), let us pursue that state in this life. The issue in this life is the pursuit of holiness not the achievement of it, which awaits our glorification.

The phrase *"without which no one will see the Lord"* refers to "the sanctification" (which is assured in the believer) not the "pursuit" (which is not an assured response). We might paraphrase the verse this way: "Since you know God has destined you to the holiness necessary for full fellowship with God, pursue it in this life as disciples of Christ. If you do not pursue holiness, God will need to correct you" (vs. 12–13).

James 2:12–13
"Judgment will be merciless"

James indicates "judgment will be merciless for those who show no mercy." The question must be asked—In which sphere of one's existence does this apply? Does it refer to the final judgment of one's soul before God, or does it refer to the social dynamic of this life. The last phrase in verse 13 *"mercy triumphs over judgment"* makes most sense if the
social sphere is in view. James is saying those who show no mercy or grace to others will tend to be treated the same way by other people. You will find a parallel message in Matthew 18:21-35.

James 2:14–26
"Faith that works"

This passage is no doubt the classic biblical text cited to challenge the doctrine of imputed righteousness. The 24th verse seems devastatingly clear—"... *a man is justified by works, and not by faith alone.*" There have been many attempted explanations and even expulsions of this text in an effort to harmonize it with Paul's teaching. It should be noted that Acts 15 and Galatians 2 indicate that Paul and his message were presented and accepted by James and the other Apostles suggesting there was no discontinuity between James and Paul. We should therefore look for a way to understand James so as to be consistent with Paul.

My explanation takes its cue from verse 14 and the phrase, "*what use is it?*" This passage is addressing the usefulness of faith especially in the affairs of this life (vs. 15–16). It is entirely possible that the "*justification*" James has in mind is not the Pauline concept of man's relationship before God but rather man's relationship *before* man. Just as the justification of Abraham by faith (Gen.15) is separated from his justification by works (Gen.22), so Paul's use of the word and James' use of the word need to be distinguished. You and I verify our faith confession before one another through our conduct (Matt.5:16) but need not do so before God who looks at the heart (Rom.4:2–3). Faith without works helps no one and is unseen by man.

Abraham's experience provides a good example of Paul's doctrine of justification by faith before God (Rom.4:3) and also justification by works before man (Jas.2:21). It also can be said that we are saved (with respect to our usefulness or fruitfulness) in this life by our actions as in the case of 1 Timothy 3:15 and 1 Corinthians 10–17. These texts and others suggest that Paul like James recognized the need to demonstrate faith *before men*. For a greater discussion of this passage go to pp 134-138.

1 Peter 1:14–19
"Judging according to each man's work"

This text seems to suggest that God will (at the final judgment) weigh every person's work in the flesh and give acceptance only to those who are as holy as God is holy. Such a reading would further force us to conclude 1) only Christ would escape condemnation because all others (including sincere believers) have sinned and do continue to fall short of God's perfect holy standard, and 2) Peter contradicts Paul and is even inconsistent within his present letter, for he affirms salvation on the basis of faith in Christ (1 Pet.1:3–5,8–9; 3:18,21).

A better understanding of this text would see it as an exhortation to believers who have been delivered from judgment (Jn.5:24) by the blood of Christ to live holy lives, not forgetting the sacrifice that delivered them (1 Pet.1:18)
.

The "impartial judgment" of God is an indication of God's assessment of sin as sin and not a reference to the condemnation rendered at the final "day of judgment." In other words, Peter is saying, "God will always see sin as sin, no matter who commits it." This is not to say all will experience the same consequences. The sinning believer will be clothed in the blood of Christ and thus *not* be condemned along with the world on the great day of final judgment (Jn.5:24; Rom.8:1).

The sinning believer will however be disciplined as a son (see Heb.12:7–13). Peter's argument is that "you (as a child of God) should recognize the sinfulness of sin because of the nature of the sacrifice required to atone for it" (vs. 18–19). He is warning his Christian readers to live so as to reflect their new family roots, and not to conclude that sin is no longer sin for them just because they are in Christ. The trials of life that befall Christians are the result of God's judgment on a fallen world. Christians do not escape this judgment, but they do have hope that is unique to them in the midst of the suffering.

1 Peter 4:17-18
"Judgment to begin with the household of God"
"it is with difficulty that the righteous is saved."

This passage suggests that the believer will face the same anxiety in the face of God's judgment as the *"unbeliever."* Note first of all that Peter is referring to the believer as "the righteous" in contrast to *"the godless man and the sinner"* (vs.18). It is possible that the judgment in view here is to be linked with the suffering (vs.19) that Christians (and others) face in a hostile culture, not the condemnation of God. There is no mention of God's judgment in this context. The righteous faces a difficult time in this life, how much more the sinner. In other words, everyone in this life will suffer (be judged) at the hands of others in one way or another but those who are not righteous will have the worst of it. Those who are holy may not escape judgment (suffering) in this life but they are to trust God and do what is right is spite of the consequences.

1 John 2:3–6
"Knowing God and keeping His commandments"

"Knowing God" is a process. To the extent we know Him, we love Him and obey Him. This text is not a statement about our salvation relationship to God in Christ by faith but rather a reference to our relative knowledge of Him. The context clearly indicates we do and will sin (1:8–2:2). In chapter 3:2, we are given the hope that we will be sinless as He is, but only when we see Him clearly and know Him fully. Until then, we are in process.

1 John 3:3–10; 5:18
"No one born of God sins"

This section suggests (at first glance) that a true believer will never sin (vs. 6,9), and if he sins, he is "of the devil" (vs. 8,10). Upon closer examination however we note two important contextual observations: 1) John assumes true believers can and will sin (1Jn.:8-2:2); 2) John also recognizes that our perfection in life awaits our perfect vision of Him, which is yet future (3:2). To the extent we "abide in Him," "*see Him*," or "*know Him*" (3:6), we will not sin. To the extent we are "*born of God*," having "*His seed abiding in us*," we cannot sin, because in Him there is no sin (vs. 5). These statements (i.e., "*begotten of God*," "*having His seed abiding in us*," "*knowing God*," etc.) are describing some-thing that is in "process." John seems to use these terms in both a completed and ongoing sense. We are abiding in Him and do know Him (2:12-14), yet we need to be exhorted to do so (2:28, 3:18, 4:7). Chapter 3:1–3 combines both present state (vs. 1) and future hope (vs. 2–3). A key word in John's writing is "*abide*." It is an active verb that can be relative in our experience, that is to say we can be at various stages of abiding just as we can be at various stages of knowing, seeing, believing, and loving. Thus we will be at various stages of sinless perfection. This text is not addressing the issue of justification but rather the issue of growth. In 1 John 5:18 Jesus is described with these words, "*He who was born of God*". In the same verse, believers are said to be "*born of God*" and in that state do not sin. The degree to which Christ's Spirit is expressed in us is the same degree to which it can be said we do not sin. The Spirit of Christ cannot sin, but the believer who is yet to be fully born of God in the sense the Spirit of Christ is formed in him can and often does sin.

John indicates that false teachers were confusing his readers (2:26). While the false teachers are not specified, there is strong evidence in John's language and arguments that the seeds of Gnostic doctrine were in mind. One aspect of Gnostic teaching was that the body was insignificant, and therefore what a believer did "in the body" was insignificant. The point John is making is that if a Christian has the authentic seed of Christ (new nature), there can be no room for justifying a life of careless sin. Sin is not compatible with the Spirit and seed of Christ.

Revelation 3:4–5
"He who overcomes will not have his name erased from the book of life"

The church in Sardis (vs.1–6) had the reputation of being spiritually alive, but it was in reality dead (vs.1). This church might be compared in the parable of the soils (Matt.13:20–21) to the rocky places, which received the Word but the temptations of the world kept it from gaining firm root. There were some in Sardis who were true believers *"overcomers"* (vs.4–5), and if the rest would repent and press on to genuine faith, they too would not be removed from the book of life. That is they would make their confession of faith real and effective. Like the Prodigal son in Luke 15 these "confessional believers" had yet to act out their faith and return home. They had a confession without the act of repentance.

Appendix #2
The Heidelberg Catechism

The Heidelberg Catechism (dating from the 16th century) is a Protestant confessional document taking the form of a series of questions and answers, for use in teaching Reformed Christian doctrine. It has been translated into many languages and is regarded as one of the most influential of the Reformed catechisms.

Question

How are you righteous before God?

Answer

Only by true faith in Jesus Christ. In spite of the fact that my conscience accuses me that I have grievously sinned against all the commandments of God, and that I have failed to keep any of them, and that I am still ever prone to all that is evil, yet God, without any merit of my own, out of pure grace, grants me the benefits of the perfect expiation of Christ, imputing to me his righteousness and holiness, as if I had never committed a single sin or had ever been sinful, having fulfilled myself all the obedience which Christ has carried out for me, if only I accept such favor with a trusting heart.

Cheap Grace and Law lite

The grace of God in Christ is in constant danger of being misrepresented by those who proclaim the gospel. First of all it can be presented as a thinly disguised message of law with a hidden demand for moral reform as a part of the package. In other words, the marquee reads FREE GRACE but the fine print says "only for those who trust AND OBEY." Such a message suggests that at the end of the day it is moral obedience that secures your relationship with God. It proclaims that God gives us a clear revelation of what holiness means in the life of Jesus and He gives us the power to obey in the Holy Spirit. This suggests that we are without excuse as He calls us to be holy as He is holy. I call this "grace lite" because it really is not grace at all. It confuses the ministry of the Holy Spirit (our comforter) with that of Jesus (our substitute).

There is a second distortion that can be made in speaking of the grace of God. This distortion equates grace with a relaxing of the standards of holiness. It suggests that God is gracious in the sense that he simply lowers or removes the moral expectations of His subjects so that they are acceptable without meeting the requirements of the holy nature of God as expressed in the law. We might call this "law lite" because it seems to ignore or look past the moral requirements of the law. What I intended to show in the first section of this book was how radical grace does not take the demands of the law too lightly. I argued that it takes the demands of the law far more seriously than those who teach that the grace of God be notarized by practiced holiness in the life of the believer. I take the standards of the law to be beyond the reach of fallen man. We hunger and thirst for a righteousness that is beyond our reach EVEN WITH THE POWER OF THE INDWELLING SPIRIT. We need the cross of Christ and its radical grace before we can have peace with God, one another, and ourselves.

Holy Sinners

The phrase "Holy Sinners" can be applied to two different individuals. It is first applied to Jesus Christ, who though holy (without sin), became a sin bearer (a sinner) for others. Secondly, it is applied to anyone who is united with Christ through faith. Such a person, while yet a sinner, is declared "holy" (justified) before God through the imputation of Christ's righteousness. The apostle Paul puts it concisely in 2 Corinthians 5:21 *"He made him who knew no sin to be sin on our behalf, so that we might become the righteousness of God in him."*

About the Author

James Owen Abrahamson is a ThM graduate of Dallas Theological Seminary and for nearly three decades has been the pastor/teacher of the Chapel Hill Bible Church near the University of North Carolina at Chapel Hill, NC. Though retired from his position at the church, he continues to preach in the Chapel Hill area, write, and teach a regular class as a part of his church family.

Jim has served as a church consultant, been a part of the adjunct faculty at UNC's continuing education in religion, and has written and contributed to several books – *Put Your Best Foot Forward* (Abingdon Press, 1994), Quest Study Bible (Zondervan, 1994), *Growing Your Church through Evangelism and Outreach* (Edited by Marshall Shelley, Moorings, 1996), *Lessons in Leadership* (Edited by Randal Roberts, 1999, Kregel), *Peace Makers* (Light Messages, 2011). He and his wife (Ceecy) have three grown children and four grandchildren.

The passion and theme of Jim's teaching has been "the grace of God" and "the power of Christ's Spirit through the teaching of Scripture" to inspire lives to peace, worship, and service. The theme and content of this book is the heart of much of what he has been saying for three decades of ministry. Jim is committed to a lifestyle of learning, modeling, and teaching to equip believers so they can live authentic Christian lives as ambassadors of God's Kingdom in this world. His website is ***apttoteach.org***. This book is the first of a two part series, which includes *Peace Makers*.

Subject Index

Scripture Index

1 Chronicles

1 Corinthians

1 John

1 Peter

1 Samuel

1 Thessalonians

1 Timothy

2 Corinthians

2 Peter

2 Thessalonians

2 Timothy

216

www.ingramcontent.com/pod-product-compliance
Lightning Source LLC
Chambersburg PA
CBHW030825090426
42737CB00009B/880